Kerr County

Texas

Divorce Records

1856-1990

Compiled by

Gloria C. Dozier

HERITAGE BOOKS
2008

HERITAGE BOOKS

AN IMPRINT OF HERITAGE BOOKS, INC.

Books, CDs, and more—Worldwide

For our listing of thousands of titles see our website
at
www.HeritageBooks.com

Published 2008 by
HERITAGE BOOKS, INC.
Publishing Division
100 Railroad Ave. #104
Westminster, Maryland 21157

Other books by the author:

Kerr County, Texas Birth Records
Kerr County, Texas Death Records, 1903-1960
Kerr County, Texas Divorce Records, 1856-1990
Kerr County, Texas Land Records, 1837-1927, Volume 1, A-K
Kerr County, Texas Land Records, 1837-1927, Volume 2, L-Z
Kerr County, Texas Probate Records, 1856-2002
Kerrville Daily Times *Obituary Books, 1986-2000, Master Index*
Kerrville Daily Times *Obituary Index, 1925-April 30, 1979*
Kerrville Mountain Sun *and* Kerrville Advance *Obituary and Death Notice Index, 1898-1965*

International Standard Book Number: 978-0-7884-3742-7

FOREWORD

This book is done in two parts since the information came from two different courts.

The first part is from the records of the 216th District Court and covers the time frame of 1856 through 1985.

The Second part is from the Kerr County Family Court records. These records cover the time frame of 1985 to 1990. Apparently, the records of the County Court and the District Court were combined in the book under the title of FAMILY COURT.

The cases with CV preceding the number are from the County Court while the District Court cases have a number followed by a letter of the alphabet.

Gloria C. Dozier
August 2007

INDEX
216th District Court Divorce Records

INDEX
Kerr County Family Court Divorce Records

Case	Plaintiff	Defendant	Date

A

Case	Plaintiff / Defendant	Date
81248a	Abbott, Carroll Patric	
	Phyllis Gail Abbott	25 Feb. 1982
88115a	Abbott, Gracie Lexie	
	Carroll Texas Abbott	19 Aug. 1988
85145a	Abel, Carol	
	Lynn DeJuan Abel	26 Oct. 1987
86108a	Abernathy, Michael Eugene	
	Jo Ann Abernathy	11 June 1986
2046	Ables, Sallie	
	Jack Ables	12 Oct. 1936
88186a	Acevedo, Lucy Lopez	
	Avelino DeLa Paz Acevedo	13 Sept. 1989
81127a	Adair, Johnny Gene	
	Patricia Ann Adair	18 Mar. 1982
5479	Adams, Herma Lee	
	Freddie Paul Adams	19 Mar. 1965
3977	Adams, Jack Charles	
	Frances F. Adams	11 Sept. 1953
5966	Adams, Judy A.	
	Billie D. Adams	25 Oct. 1967
86172a	Adams, Timothy Lee	
	Stephanie D. Adams	15 Oct. 1986
3050	Adamson, Louise	
	Alvia Adamson	25 Oct. 1946
4050	Adamik, Nellie Marie	
	Franklin Alvin Adamik	2 Apr. 1954
3619	Adley, Margaret	
	William Henry Adley	7 Sept. 1951
4377	Adrain, Erwin E.	
	Dorothy Adrain	11 Apr. 1957
1643	Adrain, Morris Joe	
	Gertrude Adrain	18 Apr. 1932
6255	Aguero, Victoria	
	Manuel R. Aguero	21 Nov. 1969
5266	Aguerro, Pedro	
	Marie Aguerro	19 Oct. 1963
78116a	Aguilar, Alma O.	
	Abel Aguilar	16 Feb. 1979

Case	Plaintiff	Defendant	Date
2650	Aguirre, E. S.		
		Rachel P. Aguirre	25 Feb. 1946
2971	Ake, Minnie		
		Jack Ake	30 May 1946
4519	Akin, Dovie		
		Charles William Akin	14 Oct. 1957
859a	Akin, Tracie Rodene		
		Kenneth Wayne Akin	28 Mar. 1985
83206a	Akin, William M.		
		Anne C. Akin	2 Dec. 1983
824a	Akshar, Abdul Kader M.		
		Zacklin Akshar	3 June 1982
2139	Albe, Wright		
		Ruth Albe	23 Mar. 1938
2749	Albe, Wright D.		
		Mae Morris Albe	25 Sept. 1944
81111a	Albrecht, Alton Emil		
		Loretta Garcia Albrecht	18 Sept. 1981
82171a	Albrecht, Teresa Jane		
		Aubrey Clinton Albrecht	19 Nov. 1982
3586	Alcorta, Indelesio		
		Mathilda Alcorta	19 Oct. 1951
7861a	Aldrich, Mildred T. Rees		
		Raymond Leslie Aldrich	3 Feb. 1979
2352	Alexander, A. L.		
		Maudie M. Alexander	20 Sept. 1939
6940	Alexander, Arlette		
		Ray Gene Alexander	12 Jan. 1978
82231a	Alexander, Dortha		
		Scott Alexander	22 Dec. 1982
5184	Alexander, James R.		
		Dorothy Jan Alexander	12 Mar. 1963
3981	Alexander, Julia Hutchinson		
		Charles Jerome Alexander	8 Sept. 1953
3360	Alexander, Ruby Lee		
		Lonnie Alexander	16 Mar. 1949
5779	Alexander, Shira Ann		
		Paul Anthony Alexander	2 Dec. 1966
1950	Alford, Sue		
		Warren Alford	15 Oct. 1935
4975	Allen, Ava Lee		
		Harry Leon Allen Sr.	3 Jan. 1962

2

Case	Plaintiff	Defendant	Date
2625	Allen, H. E.		
		Bettye C.Allen	15 Mar. 1943
8485a	Allen, Lanelle Yvonne		
		Douglas Eugene Allen	8 June 1984
911	Allen, Mike L.		
		Cora Allen	5 Apr. 1935
3197	Allerkamp, Elsa		
		William Allerkamp	------ 1947
1892	Altinn, Faye		
		Sam Altinn	23 Oct. 1934
82198a	Alvarado, Molly Ann		
		Manuel Alvarado	9 Dec. 1982
4711	Alvarado, Santos		
		Anita Alvarado	13 Mar. 1959
8028a	Alvarez, Olga Ayala		
		Reynandro Alvarez	12 May 1980
5842	Amadar, Janie		
		Severino Amadar Jr.	20 Apr. 1967
3995	Amos, James		
		Reola Amos	1 Feb. 1954
1959	Anderson, Florence		
		Tom B. Anderson	23 Oct. 1935
6202	Anderson, Ida Mae		
		Woodrow W. Anderson	9 May 1969
8262a	Anderson, Lisa Diane		
		Robt. Lynn Anderson	11 June 1982
1650	Anderson, Lois		
		A. E. Anderson	11 Apr. 1932
4354	Andrews, Barbara Jean		
		Marion Dean Andrews	14 Aug. 1956
84268a	Andrews, Bonnie Kim		
		Kevin Douglas Allen	21 Nov. 1984
4102	Antoine, Iva Jane		
		H. J. Antoine	26 July 1954
5396	Anzualda, Jacinto R.		
		Genevera Pierce Anzualda	17 Nov. 1964
88203a	Appling, Alice Ann		
		Van Jan Appling	13 Jan. 1989
6273	Armour, Katherine		
		L. E. Armour	1 Oct. 1969
5596	Armour, Lowell E.		
		Elva Mae Armour	10 Dec, 1965
3926	Arnecke, Henry L.		
		Edna Jean Arnecke	13 Apr. 1953

Case	Plaintiff	Defendant	Date
79133a	Arnold, Bonnie L.		
		Cecil Carl Arnold	29 May 1980
8048a	Arnold, Laurance M.		
		Nettie Belle Arnold	28 Oct. 1980
5950	Arnold, Mary Frances		
		Richard S. Arnold	25 Oct. 1967
6312	Arnold, Patsy		
		Charles H. Arnold	13 Jan. 1970
80253a	Arntfield, Ernest A.		
		Iona B. Arntfield	27 Jan. 1981
80113a	Arp, Billy Joe		
		Elizabeth Ann Arp	18 July 1980
85138a	Arredondo, Ernestine		
		Carlos T. Arredondo	28 Aug. 1985
4806	Arredondo, Juanta		
		Raul Arredondo	10 July 1961
8578a	Arredondo, Maria Inez		
		Raul R. Arredondo	25 June 1985
8882a	Arreola, Asuncion Martinez		
		Mamuel Arreola	6 July 1988
2446	Arreola, Avila		
		Louis Arreola	29 Oct. 1940
4967	Arreola, Reyna		
		Vincente Arreola	20 May 1961
3941	Arreola, Raul R.		
		Neomi G. Arreola	13 Aug. 1953
5163	Arroyos, Jacinto B.		
		Juanita G. Arroyos	8 Jan. 1963
82139a	Ash, Shirley A.		
		Alan A. Ash	22 Oct. 1982
1796	Ashinhurst, Agnes		
		Claude Ashinhurst	22 Apr. 1932
5489	Ashmore, Clara B.		
		Thomas J. Ashmore	30 Apr. 1965
4292	Autin, Earl O.		
		Imogene Street Austin	8 Feb. 1956
5930	Axtell, Paul Wayne		
		Barbara Lucille Axtell	29 Nov. 1967
3086	Ayala, Armando S.		
		Mary J. A. Ayala	14 Apr. 1947
87216a	Ayala, Bianca Alicia		
		Gilbert Calderon Ayala	19 Nov. 1987
6309	Ayala, Emma		
		Roy Ayala	11 Dec. 1969

Case	Plaintiff	Defendant	Date
6324	Ayala, Florence Juanita		
		Ramon Ayala	15 Dec. 1969
5369	Ayala, Gabriel D.		
		Vinenta Ruiz Ayala	10 Nov. 1964
4321	Ayala, Joaquin		
		Mary Louise Ayala	7 May 1956
2363	Ayala, Mary		
		Concencio Ayala	4 Oct. 1939
5709	Ayala, Rafela		
		Rudolph Ayala Jr.	21 Sept, 1966
4795	Ayala, Rudy		
		Raefela Ayala	7 Apr. 1960
2097	Ayala, Santana		
		Juanita Ayala	19 Apr. 1937
8528a	Ayala, Trinidad C.		
		Anastisa M. Ayala	28 Aug. 1985

B

Case	Plaintiff	Defendant	Date
80235a	Bachhofer, Nicki D.		
		Frank Bachhofer	22 Dec. 1980
4080	Bacon, Delbert		
		Nora Gulley Bacon	16 Dec. 1954
6209	Bacon, Julia Lucille		
		Joe D. Bacon	9 Apr. 1969
8841a	Bacon, Rodney		
		Martha Ann Bacon	5 May 1988
79286a	Baggett, Sherry Yvonne		
		Stanley W. Baggett	4 Aug. 1980
5040	Bailey, Charley E.		
		Carol June Bailey	20 Oct. 1961
5079	Bailey, Gertrude		
		Altus Raymond Bailey	24 July 1962
5912	Bailey, Jack Dona		
		Ima Jeanne Bailey	29 Nov. 1967
5704	Bailey, Mary Jane		
		Hugh F. Bailey	8 Aug, 1966
4885	Baker, Betty Lou		
		Eddie Baker	16 Sept. 1960
2308	Baker, Claud P.		
		Estella A. Baker	22 Sept. 1939

Case	Plaintiff	Defendant	Date
2154	Baker, E. E.		
		Anna Baker	25 Sept. 1937
4601	Baker, Emma Irene R.		
		Jack Baker	19 May 1958
3420	Baker, Ethel M.		
		Allen Roy Baker	6 Sept. 1949
3467	Baker, Eugene R.		
		Flora Pearl Baker	13 Dec. 1951
2571	Baker, Hattie		
		Earl Baker	9 Mar. 1943
5220	Baker, Helen A.		
		Giroo M. Baker	11 July 1963
3990	Baker, Jessie I.		
		Mary V. Baker	14 Sept. 1953
87161a	Baker, Vickie Sue		
		Bradford Roy Baker	16 Mar. 1985
2914	Baldwin, Annie V.		
		W. H. Baldwin	25 Feb. 1946
4742	Baldwin, Barbara Ann		
		Wm. Carlton Baldwin	22 Mar. 1959
4479	Baldwin, Minnie Etta		
		M. C. Baldwin	9 May 1958
8561a	Baldwin, Nancy M. Williamson		
		Wm. Carlton Baldwin	8 Nov. 1985
2462	Baldwin, Nettie		
		Owen Baldwin	11 Mar. 1941
2893	Baldwin, Viola		
		George Baldwin	4 Mar. 1946
6685	Ball, Iris Irene		
		T. Gene Ball	8 Mar. 1976
783a	Ball, Jan Ann		
		Douglas Porter Ball	16 Aug. 1978
3042	Ball, Mary Geraldine		
		Thomas E. Ball	25 Oct. 1946
5067	Ballard, Lavander M.		
		L. A. Ballard	5 Jan. 1962
85106a	Banhston, Cathy Leean		
		Danny Glenn Banhston	20 Dec. 1985
79260a	Banister, Hannalore		
		John R. Banister III	20 May 1981
3738	Banta, Jeanetta F.		
		C. L. Banta	8 Nov. 1951
8486a	Barcelo, Paula Laurice		
		Timothy Gregory Barcelo	8 June 1984

Case	Plaintiff	Defendant	Date
6020	Bardon, Daniel L.		
		Cara Mae Bardon	5 Aug. 1968
8583a	Barga, Leonard Leo		
		Debra Kay Barga	31 July 1985
873a	Barker, Raymond Fulton		
		Naomi Rae Barker	7 Apr. 1987
3734	Barnes, Dorothy		
		Bernard Barnes	8 Nov. 1951
7944a	Barnes, Elizabeth J.		
		David Milton Barnes	11 June 1979
5379	Barnes, Matthew Q.		
		Bessie Marie Barnes	1 June 1965
79127a	Barnes, Norma Wilcox		
		Alan Wayne Barnes	27 Nov. 1979
84324a	Barron, Debra Marye		
		Johnny E. Barron	8 Feb. 1985
5082	Bartell, Garner Gillis		
		S. M. Bartell	22 Dec. 1962
4765	Bartley, Myrtle Eva		
		W. R. Bartley	2 Sept. 1959
3361	Barton, Annie Merle		
		Jack Hy Barton	23 May 1949
5070	Barton, Elizabeth B.		
		Lloyd Barton	26 Jan. 1962
5158	Barton, Etta Mae		
		Mason A. Barton Jr.	22 Dec. 1962
3908	Bartts, Dorothy		
		Johnnie Carol Bartts	10 Feb. 1953
3504	Bass, Alta Louise		
		Wesley Bass Jr.	19 Apr. 1950
5166	Basse, Fritz C.		
		Edna Basse	8 Jan. 1963
4917	Bateman, Effie Smith		
		Guy Paul Bateman	23 May 1961
2289	Bates, Leona		
		Carter Bates	8 Mar. 1939
4123	Baucom, Pearl		
		Sterling Maxwell Baucom	6 Dec. 1954
84273a	Baxter, Marshall Eugene		
		Despina Paula Baxter	15 Oct. 1986
2836	Baxter, Raymond		
		Marjorie Baxter	8 Oct. 1945
8354a	Beadles, Murray Lucen		
		Margaret Ann Beadles	25 May 1983

Case	Plaintiff	Defendant	Date
8257a	Beagle, Twila Geneva		
		James Nichael Beagle	31 Aug. 1982
7002	Beakley, Birdie Sue		
		James Franklin Beakley	16 Mar. 1978
79256a	Beakley, Dennis		
		Susan Beakley	28 Mar. 1980
4629	Beakley, Sandra D.		
		Ernest Beakley	26 Sept. 1958
1641	Beal, Bruce A.		
		Roxie Mc Gee Beal	6 Oct. 1931
3675	Beam, Virgil		
		Mary Lou Beam	4 Sept. 1951
3423	Beasley, Joe		
		Roberta Beasley	12 Oct. 1949
3427	Beasley, Ora Lee		
		Orville H. Beasley	11 Oct. 1949
81159a	Beatty, Donna Jean		
		Albert M. Beatty	25 Feb. 1982
2988	Beaver, Beonto		
		William Beaver	20 June 1946
4140	Beaver, Bernis		
		Madge Beaver	6 Dec. 1954
2096.5	Beaver, Bessie L.		
		Billie Beaver	30 Mar. 1937
2904	Beaver, Conrada Lopez		
		Edward P. Beaver	25 Feb. 1946
4498	Beaver, Hubert H.		
		Madge E. Beaver	29 Aug. 1957
8684a	Beaver, Kevin S.		
		Shiela K. Beaver	6 Apr. 1988
1696	Beaver, Lyda Bell		
		Louis Beaver	6 Apr. 1932
79236a	Beaver, Mary Jeanette		
		David Allen Beaver	8 Jan. 1980
5416	Beaver, Stanley N.		
		Lana Geeslin Beaver	10 Nov. 1964
5684	Beavers, James O.		
		Lola L. Beavers	19 May 1966
5830	Beck, Harley B.		
		Rose L. Beck	21 Sept. 1967
82237a	Beck, Lorraine Marie		
		William Edwin Beck	19 Aug. 1983
6966	Beckel, April Michelle		
		Ralph Chapin Beckel	8 Dec. 1977

Case	Plaintiff	Defendant	Date
84210a	Becker, Rosemary		
		Henry Becker, Jr.	18 Jan. 1985
85299a	Beckman, Kenneth Bruce		
		Karen Lynn Beckman	1 Oct. 1986
6187	Behrens, David H.		
		Shirley Mae Behrens	20 Feb. 1969
81261a	Behrens, Sandra Gail		
		Frankie James Behrens	6 Feb. 1981
83143a	Belfield, Pamela V.		
		Donald J. Belfield	22 Aug. 1983
4852	Bell, Lou Ann		
		Rex Galen Bell	6 June 1960
8532a	Belluomani, Iris Duncan		
		Adolph Lawrence Belluomani	
			21 Mar. 1986
85257a	Belnoski, Rhonda Ann		
		James Edward Belnoski	19 Dec. 1985
1658	Bendt, Henry H.		
		Clara Bendt	7 Oct. 1931
6889	Benfer, Ann Bruce		
		Eugene Louis Benfer	30 May 1978
7974a	Benevides, Linda M.		
		Johnny L. Benevides	30 Apr. 1980
5496	Benjamin, Florence B.		
		Willie Benjamin	8 Aug. 1966
5916	Benner, Elsie		
		Earl E. Benner	25 May 1967
2538	Bennett, Birdie		
		F. Bennett	16 Dec. 1941
3114	Bennett, Eulalea		
		Tony Bennett	14 Apr. 1947
85321a	Bennett, Jules E.		
		Linda M. Bennett	3 July 1986
856a	Bennett, Lois Mae		
		Virgil Lee Bennett	9 Apr. 1985
4097	Bennett, Lola C.		
		Herbert Bennett	26 July 1954
1809	Benskin, George		
		Vera Benskin	26 Oct. 1933
1860	Benson, Annie		
		W. G. Benson	17 Apr. 1934
81188a	Benson, Cynthia D.		
		John K. Benson	12 Nov. 1981

9

Case	Plaintiff	Defendant	Date
4069	Benson, Edna		
		Robert Shannon Benson	26 July 1954
5578	Benson, George W.		
		Lula Benson	6 Nov. 1965
6234	Benson, George W.		
		Minnie Benson	20 May 1969
4224	Benson, Johnie L.		
		Dorothy Marie Benson	12 Aug. 1955
2450	Benson, Johnnie		
		Mary Benson	30 Oct. 1940
4994	Benson, Johnnie L.		
		Mildred Irene Marzek Benson	
			7 June 1961
4355	Benson, Josie B.		
		George Benson	22 Sept. 1955
2884	Benson, Shannon		
		Bernice Benson	10 Dec. 1945
1564	Benson, W. G.		
		Dora Benson	4 Apr. 1932
8595a	Benson, Yvonne Janney		
		Wm. Geo. Benson II	3 July 1985
88111a	Berg, Jemmifer Aaron		
		Michael David Berg	31 Aug. 1988
84331a	Berkman, C. J.		
		Cynthia Ann Berkman	8 Feb. 1985
88144a	Bernard, Frankie/Francis		
		Kimberley Renee Bernard	15 Mar. 1989
1913	Bernhard, Mary		
		Arno Bernhard	19 Apr. 1935
2167	Bernhard, Mary		
		Arno Bernhard	38 Mar. 1939
82162a	Bevers, Bertha M.		
		Bill Bevers	22 Oct. 1982
83134a	Bevers, Bill		
		Bertha M. Beavers	18 Aug. 1983
2927	Bevershansen, Violet		
		Wm. Bevershansen	25 Feb. 1946
2705	Bibbee, Arthur		
		Sybil Bibbee	11 Oct. 1944
79282a	Biermann, Joseph M.		
		Janie Marie Biermann	20 Fev. 1980
1951	Bierschwale, Dewitt		
		Dorris Ruth Bierschwale	9 Oct. 1935

Case	Plaintiff	Defendant	Date
2882	Bierschwale, M. R.		
		Gladys Bierschwale	13 Nov. 1945
5812	Bierschwale, Mary		
		John Wm. Bierschwale	16 Jan. 1967
2388	Bierschwale, Mineola		
		Dewitt Bierschwale	5 Mar. 1940
2619	Bill, Alberto		
		Gorgina R. Bill	2 Apr. 1943
4973	Bill, Concha		
		Alberto Bill	30 June 1961
6154	Bill, Francesca P.		
		Alfredo Bill	16 Dec. 1968
803a	Bingham, Eula		
		Horace C. Bingham	24 July 1980
4891	Binion, F. W.		
		Mattie B. Binion	16 Sept. 1960
82193a	Bird, Kim Ellen		
		Gary Wayne Bird	21 Mar. 1983
5034	Birdwell, Kathleen Koehler		
		Clifford La Fayette Birdwell	
			16 Jan. 1962
84183a	Bishop, Concepcion		
		Robert Bishop	15 Mar. 1985
83143a	Bishop, Cynthia Ann		
		Ronald Bishop	2 Dec. 1983
82206a	Bishop, Gloria Frank		
		Vernon Emil Bishop	8 May 1984
2788	Bishop, Manuel		
		Annie Bishop	5 Apr. 1945
5557	Bishop, Minnie Ola		
		Verdo Bishop	9 Dec, 1965
2173	Bishop, Pearl		
		Louis Bishop	8 Mar. 1938
2392	Black, Allen		
		Geneva Black	27 Mar. 1940
2752	Black, Gussie M.		
		James E. Black	19 Dec. 1944
6313	Black, Valerie Ann		
		Billy Joe Black	14 Jan. 1970
84116a	Blackburn, LeQuita Jo		
		Louis Manton Blackburn	26 July 1984
2050	Blakely, Rufus C.		
		Ada Blakely	17 Oct. 1936

Case	Plaintiff	Defendant	Date
1830	Blalock, Louis		
		Adelle Blalock	28 Mar. 1934
82125a	Bland, Alan Roe		
		Connie Deborah K. Bland	8 Oct. 1982
88250a	Blandy, Karen D.		
		Christopher N. Blandy	2 May 1989
2458	Blanks, Joe Jr.		
		Priscilla Blanks	31 Sept. 1941
81137a	Blanks, Linda Susan		
		Keith Raymond Blanks	3 Nov. 1981
5788	Blendin, Barbara Nell		
		Don Allen Blendin	8 Dec. 1966
2459	Blevins, Charlie Thos.		
		Allie Lee Blevins	18 Sept. 1941
6161	Blevins, Dalene		
		Creed N. Blevins	10 Feb. 1969
87290a	Blevins, Joseph Kyle		
		Kristen Rene Livingston Blevins	2 Mar. 1988
2997	Blevins, Mary Ann		
		Maxie Blevins	23 July 1946
1647	Blockman, Corene		
		Tom Blockman	17 Oct. 1931
6226	Blott, Juanita Fay		
		George Robert Blott	15 May 1969
2252	Blount, Milton		
		Connie Blount	8 Mar. 1939
3771	Boatwright, James S.		
		Josephine Marie Boatwright	17 Apr. 1952
4209	Bobbitt, Elizabeth		
		Wm. Sherman Bobbitt	11 May 1955
2044	Bobineaux, Inez		
		Johnnie Bobineaux	7 Oct. 1936
5497	Bocock, Jane Nees		
		Charles William Bocock III	8 June 1965
4763	Bode, Milton		
		Inez Bode	7 Aug. 1959
2330	Boechmann, E. N. Jr.		
		Patricia A. Boechmann	19 Sept. 1936
3609	Boerner, Annie V.		
		W. N. Boerner	29 Jan. 1951

Case	Plaintiff	Defendant	Date
5462	Bogle, Bobbie R.		
		J. G. Bogle Jr.	4 Mar. 1965
1637	Bolin, A. F.		
		Myette Bolin	6 Oct. 1931
3301	Bondreaux, Bertha		
		Lucius Bondreaux	25 Oct. 1948
3195	Bonn, Margaret Ann		
		Hy W. Bonn	6 Nov. 1947
85179a	Bonnet, Mary Kathryn		
		John Glenn Bonnet	8 May 1986
5558	Bonura, Faye M.		
		Sam J. Bonura	18 Jan. 1966
2701	Booth, John L.		
		Eddie Lee Booth	18 May 1944
6127	Borchers, Frances C.		
		Chester H. Borchers	4 Jan. 1969
8671a	Borchers, Linda Louise		
		Robert Martin Borchers	5 June 1985
2108	Border, Zelma		
		John Border	19 Apr. 1937
2604	Borders, Eugenia B.		
		A. B. Borders	9 Mar. 1943
86219a	Borkowski, Jackie Lee		
		Helmut George Borkowski	17 Dec. 1986
4688	Bostic, Jo Ann		
		Elton Bostic	14 Sept. 1959
5917	Boudreaux, Pauline C.		
		George A. Boudreaux	8 Aug. 1967
6148	Bourke, Mary Sue		
		Jack O. Bourke	19 Mar. 1969
3410	Bourke, Myrel Hardin		
		Jack A. Bourke	6 Sept. 1949
3083	Bower, William F.		
		Mamie R. Bower	28 Mar. 1947
2837	Bowers, Mary Jane		
		Otis R. Bowers	16 Sept. 1945
2630	Bowers, O. R.		
		Selma Bowers	8 Mar. 1943
8454a	Bowles, Ann E.		
		John M. Bowles	26 Apr. 1984
4599	Bowlus, Mary Jane		
		Noble Russell Bowlus	9 May 1958
4527	Bowman, Lucille White		
		Warner Lee Bowman	27 Oct. 1958

Case	Plaintiff	Defendant	Date
3250	Bowman, Treatha		
		Lester Bowman	14 June 1948
1642	Box, Golda		
		A. (E.) C. Box	6 Oct. 1931
3440	Boyd, Bertha Lee		
		Jimmie Boyd	12 Oct. 1949
3226	Boyd, John		
		Lulu Boyd	14 June 1948
81156a	Boyett, Gail Randel		
		Thomas Boyett Jr.	2 Nov. 1981
3075	Boyles, Virginia		
		Merle Boyles	10 June 1947
2340	Braden, Thetis		
		David P. Braden	19 Sept. 1939
4085	Bradford, Chloe		
		Joe Lynn Bradford	26 July 1954
1838	Brady, Mrs. Tullie		
		Claud Brady	27 Mar. 1934
1938	Brady, Winnie		
		Walter Brady	8 Oct. 1936
3136	Brailey, Catherine M.		
		Munsen H. Brailey	9 June 1947
5884	Branch, Sedalia Frances		
		Horace Branch	29 June 1967
8190a	Branch, Sharon Ann		
		Truman D. Branch	31 July 1981
4924	Brandon, Loretta		
		James Edward Brandon	23 Nov. 1960
3491	Brandt, Earl C.		
		Winifred Brandt	6 Feb. 1950
6871	Brasher, Lynn W.		
		Wilma E. Brasher	29 Aug. 1977
4547	Bratcher, Eula Mae		
		Charels B. Bratcher	5 Aug. 1958
2821	Braun, Anthony		
		Dorothy Braun	10 Dec. 1945
3000	Bray, Calvin C.		
		Clara Bray	3 Sept. 1946
4064	Braziel, Arnicia		
		Tommie Braziel	7 Feb. 1955
82138a	Bremseth, Margaret Eileen		
		Michael Dale Bremseth	8 Oct. 1982
8670a	Bressie, Lorraine Margaret		
		Ronald Bressie	11 July 1986

Case	Plaintiff	Defendant	Date
88183a	Bridges, Frances Elrod		
		Wm. Oliver Bridges	16 Nov. 1988
8452a	Bridges, Ida Mae		
		James Richard Bridges	10 May 1984
4732	Bridges, Lena Mae Ross		
		Allen Bridges	6 May 1959
79134a	Bridges, Terri Kay		
		James R. Bridges	6 Mar. 1980
5669	Briggs, Nellie Faye		
		Thomas J. Briggs	17 Sept. 1966
6566	Brinkman, Sidney		
		L. O. Brinkman	2 Oct. 1972
3923	Bristol, Margaret		
		J. N. Bristol	13 Apr. 1953
2103	Britt, Wanda Lee		
		Gabriel Britt	30 Mar. 1937
81171a	Brondo, Marlene Vernell		
		Richard Roger Brondo	5 Nov. 1981
3362	Brooks, Beatrice		
		Chas. E. L. Brooks	13 Oct. 1949
3337	Brooks, C. S.		
		Mozelle Brooks	20 Dec. 1948
3034	Brooks, Ellen M.		
		Glen E. Brooks	29 Oct. 1946
2763	Brooks, Vera		
		Homer Brooks	19 Dec. 1944
84143a	Brothers, Rachel Moreno		
		Steven Michael Brothers	25 Oct. 1984
1812	Brown, Ada		
		Robert Brown	28 Oct. 1933
2073	Brown, Aileen		
		Felton Brown	16 Oct. 1936
1960	Brown, Andrew L.		
		Hattie Mae Brown	21 Oct. 1935
3752	Brown, Billie Jean		
		Cecil Dayton Brown	11 Feb. 1952
3087	Brown, Doris L.		
		Frank Brown	14 Apr. 1947
2781	Brown, Edna Opal		
		John Henry Brown	5 Apr. 1945
5181	Brown, Gloria Carmeleta		
		Ardis P. Brown Jr.	21 Mar. 1963
1651	Brown, John H.		
		Mary Brown	24 Oct. 1931

Case	Plaintiff	Defendant	Date
6006	Brown, John William		
		Roberta R. Brown	24 June 1968
4338	Brown, Ruby		
		J. R. Brown	10 July 1956
1799	Brown, Sallie		
		Willie Brown	27 Oct. 1933
2486	Brown, Sammie		
		Christine Brown	26 Sept. 1941
80201a	Brown, Spencer		
		Linda Brown	18 Dec. 1980
1965	Brown, Willis		
		Lola Brown	6 Apr. 1936
8776a	Brownson, Frederick Oscar		
		Carol Lynn Cammack Brownson	11 June 1987
4403	Brumley, Aubrey		
		Orelle Brown Brumely	16 Apr. 1957
4505	Brummett, Lena May		
		Walter Raymond Brummett	10 Sept. 1957
2481	Bryan, B. W.		
		Ruby Bryan	27 Sept. 1941
1723	Bryden, Starr		
		Myrtle Bryden	20 Oct. 1932
8295a	Buck, Camilla Neece		
		David Michael Buck	21 Dec. 1982
5766	Buck, Charles Edward		
		Sandra Sue Buck	21 Oct. 1966
80128a	Buck, Leslie Ann		
		Mern Louis Buck	30 July 1980
82281a	Buckman, James Henry		
		Alcyone Buckman	25 Feb. 1983
2829	Buford, Myrtle B.		
		Freeman W. Buford	27 July 1945
82240a	Bullock, Donald D.		
		Sharon Kay Bullock	6 Jan. 1982
8741a	Bulta, Ray A.		
		Marie Crocker Bulta	4 Nov. 1987
8598a	Bunch, Bernice W.		
		Harold H. Bunch	11 July 1985
83191a	Bundick, Gary D.		
		Vickie Storms Bundick	12 Dec. 183
3654	Bundick, Juanita C.		
		Eugene Laurence Bundick	26 Apr. 1951

Case	Plaintiff	Defendant	Date
1933	Bundick, Laura		
		Louis Bundick	15 Oct. 1935
782a	Bundy, Irma Jean Sophia Dell		
		Glen Louis Bundy	4 Aug. 199978
4450	Burgess, Delbert G.		
		Draxie Minnie Burgess	4 June 1957
84264a	Burgess, Pamela C.		
		Nickey D. Burgess	5 Dec. 1984
4682	Burgin, Barbara H.		
		Wilfred Sherman Burgin	7 Jan. 1959
3905	Burkhart, Fred G.		
		Cora M. Burkhart	14 July 1953
3902	Burleson, Alfred		
		Velma Burleson	2 Feb. 1953
2716	Burleson, Erna		
		Alfred Burleson	18 May 1944
2102	Burleson, J. H.		
		Melissie Burleson	30 Mar. 1937
2114	Burnett, Elma Dell		
		Georgia Burnett	19 Apr. 1937
4206	Burnett, Lillian Irene		
		Jack Burnett	12 Aug, 1955
2280	Burnett, Mildred		
		E. D. Burnett	27 Mar. 1939
2854	Burns, Anna		
		Hilbeard Burns	14 Sept. 1945
2879	Burns, Daniel L. Jr.		
		Sallie J. Burns	20 June 1945
6528	Burns, Dorothy Lee		
		Ralph N. Burns	5 Mar. 1972
2496	Burrer, Lois		
		Melton C. Burrer	16 Sept. 1941
84291a	Burrow, Tresa Kay		
		Timothy Ray Burrow	9 Jan. 1985
3462	Burt, Lola		
		B. H. Burt	12 Dec. 1949
3251	Burton, Lou Ellen		
		P. J. Burton	14 June 1948
5230	Busby, Mary Sue		
		Paul Busby	15 June 1964
4932	Bush, Reone A.		
		W. D. Bush	23 Nov. 1960
4794	Butler, Bobby		
		Christine B. Butler	23 Nov. 1959

Case	Plaintiff	Defendant	Date
5639	Butler, Bobby		
		Mary Jane Butler	1 Apr. 1966
1853	Butler, Harrison H.		
		Mary Butler	21 Oct. 1935
8317a	Butler, Jesusa D.		
		Frances C. Butler	24 Mar. 1983
6116	Byerly, Linda Georgann		
		Robert Earl Byerly	18 Oct. 1968
2	Byfield, Elizabeth		
		William Byfield	29 Nov. 1871
2362	Byrd, Alis		
		Sam H. Byrd	5 Oct. 1939
4331	Byrd, Viola		
		Troy Byrd	5 June 1956

C

Case	Plaintiff	Defendant	Date
80130a	Cabrera, Gloria Ann		
		Mariano Cabrera Jr.	28 Oct. 1980
4253	Cade, Charles		
		Joyce Louise Cade	5 Oct. 1955
4343	Cade, Louise		
		Marion Cade	10 July 1956
4131	Cade, Marie		
		William A. Cade	6 Dec. 1954
4200	Cade, Nellie Frances		
		Marion Cade	11 May 1955
3166	Cade, Willie A.		
		Lila Isabel Cade	4 Sept. 1947
5215	Cahill, Arlice Irene		
		Willard Thos. Cahill	3 Aug. 1964
3115	Cahill, Rosemary		
		Douglas Cahill	14 Apr. 1947
2053	Cairnes, Minnie		
		J. W. Cairnes	6 Oct. 1936
4866	Caldron, Estella		
		Alfonso Caldron	7 June 1960
2174	Calk, Velma		
		Earl B. Calk	29 Nov. 1937
2928	Callahan, Myrtle		
		Harley Callahan	25 Feb. 1946
81119a	Callaway, Beverly Charlene		
		Randy Carroll Callaway	7 Jan. 1982

Case	Plaintiff	Defendant	Date
8420a	Callozo, Stella Faye		
		Isaac G. Callozo	6 Apr. 1984
8649a	Calvert, Wilton Ralph		
		Judith Ann Calvert	17 Oct. 1986
3939	Camano, Adela		
		Frank Camano	14 July 1953
79	Campos, Thomas		
		Barbara Campos	23 Mar. 1878
4918	Canady, Elmarie Henderson		
		L. V. Canady	19 Dec. 1960
8090a	Caniff, Ruby		
		Dale Caniff	22 Feb. 1984
6350	Cantu, Eva B.		
		Jose A. Cantu	1 June 1970
6866	Cantu, Margaret Santos		
		Hector Deleon Cantu	7 Sept. 1977
5658	Cantwell, Cynthia Dickey		
		Jasper L. Cantwell	19 May 1966
2353	Carabajahal, Lena M.		
		Dolores Carabajahal	20 Sept. 1939
2020	Carabajahal, Santos		
		Cuca Carabajahal	18 Sept. 1939
2809	Carabajahal, Victoriana M.		
		Guadalupe Carabajahal	8 June 1945
3378	Carazus, Magdalene		
		Elmo Carazus	17 Mar. 1949
83142a	Carey, Margaret Coffey		
		Jack W. Carey	6 Sept. 1983
7983a	Caribardi, Herbert F.		
		Barbara R. D. Caribardi	5 July 1979
85141a	Carlile, Cara Mae		
		Tommy Ralph Carlile	28 Aug. 1985
4172	Carlile, Mildred		
		Frank M. Carlile	12 Aug. 1955
815a	Carlisle, Wm. Ernest		
		Beverly Virginia Carlisle	23 Mar. 1981
84171a	Carlos, Sue F.		
		Rosalio M. Carlos	16 Aug. 1984
3314	Carlson, Marion M.		
		Leonard O. Carlson	25 Oct. 1948
82245a	Carnahan, Chas. Alan		
		Ellen Lulu Carnahan	12 July 1983

Case	Plaintiff	Defendant	Date
2082	Carnes, Elsie		
		John Carnes	7 Oct. 1937
2993	Carnes, Frances M.		
		John M. Carnes	20 June 1946
3274	Carnes, H. C.		
		Dorothea Lou Carnes	29 July 1948
86135a	Carpio, Angelo		
		Linda Irene Carpio	29 July 1986
5206	Carr, Edna Jo		
		Thomas E. Carr	5 June 1963
3868	Carr, Frances		
		Alvin D. Carr	16 Apr. 1953
4196	Carr, Julia Marie Wright		
		Carl Edward Carr	5 Nov. 1955
5485	Carr, Sandra Sue		
		William Monroe Carr	13 Aug. 1965
3610	Carr, Wayne		
		Bettye Jo	30 Jan 1951
6430	Carreon, Jose		
		Guadalupe Carreon	22 June 1970
88162a	Carrillo, Mary Christine		
		Jesue Arnulfo Carrillo	5 Oct. 1988
4094	Carringtono, Genia Mae		
		Robt. L. Carrington	26 July 1954
84224a	Carroll, Joyce Ann		
		Matthew Clinton Carroll	25 Oct. 1984
80240a	Carroll, Kay Leann		
		Chas. Elvis Carroll	23 Dec. 1980
82152a	Carroll, Nancy S.		
		Matthew C. Carroll	28 Apr. 1983
83189a	Carroll, Ronnie L.		
		Patricia Diane Carroll	2 Dec. 1983
2056	Carson, Hilda		
		Jno. Carson	10 Oct. 1936
3186	Carson, Junior		
		Dorothy H. Carson	15 Dec. 1947
4054	Carson, Junior		
		Valerie A. Carson	2 Apr. 1954
85144a	Carson, Martha Rose		
		Ross Clarence Carson	28 Aug. 1985
2185	Carson, Mary E.		
		Joe F. Carson	8 Mar. 1938
3540	Carson, Mary Jo		
		J. R. Carson	25 Aug. 1950

Case	Plaintiff	Defendant	Date
3850	Casey, Winnie Austin Charles E. Casey		15 Dec. 1952
80130a	Caskey, Wanda Sue James Dow Caskey		18 Sept. 1980
5910	Cason, Isabel John Raymond Cason		21 Mar. 1968
3806	Cason, Maggie Nugent Cason		5 Aug. 1952
4564	Cason, Patsy J. C. Cason		14 Feb. 1958
83106a	Cason, Verne E. Ethmer Nugent Cason		12 July 1983
82151a	Cass, Mary Lanetta Mahaffey Wesley June Cass		28 Dec, 1982
5547	Cassell, Louise Frida James Riley Cassell		23 Aug. 1965
83180a	Castillo, Alma G. Pablo M. Castillo		4 Oct. 1983
3544	Castillo, Emelia Jose Castillo		4 Sept. 1952
85103a	Castillo, Eustolio G. Socorro Garcia Castillo		28 Aug. 1985
1792	Castillo, Jose Enriquita S. Castillo		12 Oct. 1932
2140	Castillo, Juan Catrina Castillo		22 Sept. 1937
3177	Castillo, Juanita Juan B. Castillo		6 Nov. 1947
2617	Castillo, Thomasa Gillermo Castillo		9 Nov. 1942
85302a	Castleberry, Sue Beth Lewis Laurance Riley Castleberry		13 Feb. 1986
2197	Cavness, Lucy B. John D. Cavness		28 Sept. 1938
5640	Cavness, Phil Carimino Columbo Cavness		7 June 1966
3626	Cavness, Ruby E. J. D. Cavness		25 Apr. 1951
5926	Center, Eunice Marie Jack Lee Center		8 Sept. 1967
2874	Cervantes, Domingo Maximina Cervantes		2 Jan. 1945

Case	Plaintiff	Defendant	Date
85169a	Chacon, Hermelinda		
		Joe Henry Chacon	27 Sept. 1985
5012a	Chacon, Mary Ann		
		Henry Chacon	19 Sept. 1961
7017	Chacon, Serapia		
		Steve Trevino Chacon	23 May 1978
78119a	Chadwick, Alice Ann		
		Billy Moore Chadwick	21 Dec. 1978
8227a	Chamberlain, Michael		
		Marianne Chamberlain	5 Aug. 1982
88179a	Chambers, Judy K.		
		Jeffery D. Chambers	27 Jan. 1989
5862	Chambliss, Carrie Lee		
		Donald Edgar Chambliss	18 May 1967
3203	Chambliss, Joe Lene		
		Donald E. Chambliss	15 Dec. 1947
5679	Chambliss, Lana M.		
		Donald E. Chambliss	7 July 1966
4749	Chambliss, Charlotte Joy Clark		
		Donald Edgar Chambliss	27 June 1959
4236	Chaney, Alicia		
		Thelbert C. Chaney	12 Aug. 1955
5859	Chaney, Barbara		
		Eugene Walter Chaney	13 Oct. 1967
4433	Chaney, Thelbert Charles		
		Mary Flores Chaney	18 Jan. 1957
88146a	Chapa, Maria Florinda		
		Rafael Chapa Jr.	7 Sept. 1988
6274	Chapman, Gary R.		
		Joyce F. Chapman	3 Oct. 1969
2523	Chaudoin, Ira Dell		
		B. A. Chaudoin	29 Sept. 1941
5445	Cheek, Corinne D.		
		Auburn C. Cheek	7 Jan. 1965
6367	Chenault, Frances		
		Wm. Bryan Chenault	21 Apr. 1972
8267a	Cherbonnier, Beverly A.		
		Lawrence Michael Cherbonnier	
			10 Dec. 1982
1726	Cherry, Jessie		
		Morris F. Cherry	4 Oct. 1932
2657	Chipman, Alice		
		Ernest Chipman	15 Sept. 1943

22

Case	Plaintiff Defendant	Date
7941a	Chipman, Donald C. Gaylis A. Chipman	26 July 1979
85211a	Chipman, Geneva Ernest Chipman	11 Oct. 1985
4781	Chisum, Jewel Isum Chisum	9 July 1960
84174a	Chisum, Margaret Ann Parman Billy Ray Chisum	30 Aug. 1984
4100	Cissell, Johnny B. Gloria Cissell	13 Sept. 1954
81139a	Clark, Brooks Vanna Lynn Cooper	18 Sept. 1981
4558	Clark, Hazel Abbott Vurden C. Clark	10 Jan. 1958
6986	Clark, Kathryn Smith Daigle Harry Jay Clark	2 Feb. 1978
5136	Clark, Kitty Irene Randall Clark	7 Mar. 1963
83123a	Clark, Lenora James Lewis Clark	15 Sept. 1983
87256a	Clark, Linda Perez Henry Clark Jr.	7 Apr. 1988
8272a	Clark, Mary Ann Carl Eugene Clark	23 July 1982
8854a	Clark, Michael F. Sheila C. Clark	10 Feb. 1989
86152a	Clark, Vera May Isaac Mason Clark	4 Mar. 1987
4938	Clark, Wanda E. E. Clark	16 June 1961
84314a	Clarkson, Austin Edward II Lelia Diane Clarkson	9 Jan. 1985
4399	Claypool, Harry A. Phyllis A. Claypool	17 Dec. 1956
3745	Claypool, Harry I. Grace Claypool	26 May 1952
8355a	Clement, Betty Jo John Arthur Clement	25 May 1983
5803	Clement, John A. Catherine Booth Clement	16 Jan. 1967
7033	Clements, Evelyn Pearce Chapman Waddell Clements	21 July 1978
5753	Clendenan, Leah Marlene Aubrey Watson Clendenan	21 Oct. 1966

Case	Plaintiff	Defendant	Date
5184	Clendennan, A. W.		
		Mildred Clendennan	7 Mar. 1963
6374	Clower, Billy B.		
		Mary Jane Clower	17 June 1970
4352	Cobb, Ira Morris		
		Edna Mae Cobb	6 Aug. 1956
5380	Cobb, Judy Whorton		
		Hubbard D. Cobb	1 Sept. 1964
3324	Cobb, William E.		
		Martha May Cobb	22 Nov. 1948
7053	Cochenour, Janet Marie		
		Gerry Forest Cochenour	17 Nov. 1978
6123	Cochran, Carol R.		
		Eddie H. Cochran	24 Mar. 1969
5015a	Cochran, Eddie H.		
		Jo Ann Cochran	30 Oct. 1961
88196a	Cochran, Sandra Bingaman		
		Gary Earl Cochran	13 Jan. 1989
8581a	Cockreft, Dura Kay		
		Chad Edward Cockreft	5 June 1985
1718	Coke, B. L.		
		Viola Coke	4 Oct. 1932
85222a	Coker, Collene M.		
		Glenn B. Coker	22 Oct. 1985
3544	Colazo, Faustino		
		Martha Collazo	28 Nov. 1950
86125a	Colbath, James Edward		
		Suzanne Colbath	15 Oct. 1986
1650	Colbath, Vera		
		Guy Colbath	6 Oct. 1931
1898	Colbath, Guy		
		Vera Colbath	26 Oct. 1934
86112a	Colburn, Deryl Graham		
		Deborah Perkins Colburn	18 June 1986
7836a	Coldwell, Neal Vernon		
		Sandra Jean Holmes Coldwell	
			26 Nov. 1979
8268a	Coleman, Bessie Fifer		
		Donald Ray Coleman	9 Sept. 1982
4198	Coleman, Charlie		
		Ruth Coleman	11 May 1955
2264	Coleman, E. H.		
		Belle Coleman	10 Mar. 1939

Case	Plaintiff / Defendant	Date
2866	Coleman, Lola Lester D. Coleman	10 Sept. 1945
85214a	Coleman, Shirley Ann Jerry Ray Coleman	8 Nov. 1985
2932	Collazo, Epifanio S. Mary M. Collazo	4 Mar. 1946
2064	Collazo, Faustino Cruze Lopez Collazo	10 Oct. 1936
3413	Collazo, Faustino Margaret Collazo	12 Dec. 1949
2793	Collazo, Frances Epifanio Collazo	25 May 1945
79115a	Coleman, Kenneth R. Patricia N. Coleman	31 July 1981
6910	Collier, Jeanette Marie John Thomas Collier	29 Nov. 1977
8756a	Collins, Chas. Winston Heddy Archer Collins	13 May 1987
4952	Collins, Juanita Fay Chas. Thos. Collins	10 Mar. 1961
83125a	Collyns, Grant Hartwell Debbie Marie Zinax Collyns	18 Aug. 1983
86269a	Colvin, Ellis B. Clara Dickson Colvin	21 Jan. 1987
5853	Combs, Phyllis Ann David Lee Combs	10 Aug. 1967
5735	Compton, W. D. Ruby M. Compton	21 Oct. 1966
6108	Condon, Fay L. Larry James Condon	3 Mar. 1969
81253a	Constante, Eva Bill Alejandro Lara Constante	22 Feb. 1982
4881	Contreras, Clara Juan Contreras	15 Aug. 1960
4766	Conway, Velma Louise Billie Wayne Conway 1	14 Sept, 1959
6192	Cook, Biddie Joe James Marshall Cook	26 Aug. 1970
82262a	Cook, Michael Leford Sharon Eliz. Cook	3 Feb. 1983
8778a	Cooksey, Lance Clare Marie Cooksey	10 June 1987

Case	Plaintiff Defendant	Date
2400	Cooksey, Myrtle	
	James Cooksey	29 Mar. 1940
81125a	Cooper, Edith Nell	
	Donald E. Cooper	23 Nov. 1981
83232a	Cooper, Ruth H.	
	Manly W. Cooper Jr.	14 Oct. 1986
84212a	Cordova, Felix Meja	
	Gloria Gomez Cordova	21 Nov. 1984
81100a	Cormier, Violet Lester	
	Eloi Cormier	21 Aug. 1981
299	Corn, Sarah A.	
	Lee B. Corn	11 Oct. 1891
4552	Cornett, Inez	
	Jesse M. Cornett	4 Mar. 1958
5450	Coronado, Connie J.	
	Alfredo Coronado	13 Jan. 1965
7816a	Coronado, Dorothy Jean	
	Jose Felipe Coronado	14 Oct. 1978
4807	Corpaw, Lillian	
	Robert Corpaw	6 June 1960
2213	Cortez, Estafana	
	Jesus Cortez	6 Oct. 1938
1881	Cortez, Joe	
	Ginoveba Cortez	26 Oct. 1934
3266	Cortez, Maria M.	
	Jesus Cortez	8 Sept. 1948
2530	Cottle, Carrol R.	
	Patsy Mary Cottle	16 Nov. 1941
3300	Cotton, Minnie L.	
	Richard L. Cotton	8 Sept. 1948
7007	Couch, Montye Canon	
	Cecil Carroll Couch	22 Mar. 1978
4095	Couch, Shirley Scott	
	Lloyd Couch	13 Sept. 1954
2297	Coulter, Nell	
	Fred Coulter	7 Mar. 1939
3340	Council, W. L.	
	Betty L. Council	20 Dec. 1948
87182a	Courtaway, Deborah Louise Saylor	
	Glen Paul Courtaway	7 Dec. 1988
5901	Courtney, Sandra S.	
	Ed M. Courtney	21 Aug. 1967
7977a	Courvelle, Karen Faye	
	Ronald T. Courvelle	15 Aug. 1979

Case	Plaintiff	Defendant	Date
3842	Covert, Estelle Oscar Covert		9 Feb. 1953
1662	Covert, Oscar Mildred Covert		6 Oct. 1931
1692	Covert, Oscar Mildred Covert		19 Apr. 1932
2667	Covert, Sybil C. C. Covert		15 Sept. 1943
7008	Covey, Larell Powell Floyd Edward Covey		28 Feb. 1978
6977	Cowden, Sammy Jon Gayle Ann Davis Frazier		10 Jan. 1979
79206a	Cowen, Loid Elaine Glendon Cowen		21 Dec. 1979
87295a	Cowen, Susan Marie Hugh Nolan Cowen		28 Dec. 1988
2756	Cowles, Melissa Jane W. K. Cowles		19 Dec. 1944
2188	Cowsert, Martha R. Charles A. Cowsert		8 Mar. 1938
6143	Cox, Anita L. Otis E. Cox		15 Nov. 1968
4480	Cox, Ann Ruth Claude Alvin Cox		8 July 1957
3916	Cox, Annie John H. Cox		13 Apr. 1953
5057	Cox, Barbara Ann Samuel Lee Cox		28 Feb. 1962
80249a	Cox, Gregory Lee Cindy Renee Cox		27 Jan. 1981
8734a	Cox, Jay B. Supa T. Cox		6 Jan. 1988
86253a	Cox, Johnny Lee Sheril Renee Cox		24 Nov. 1986
8328a	Cox, Kristi Rene Timothy Pruitt Cox		5 May 1983
2730	Cox, Nora Bell Welton Cox		21 Aug. 1944
6373	Cox, Pauline C. Horace E. Cox		27 Mar. 1970
4152	Cox, Ruby Seymour F. Cox		15 Dec. 1954
2933	Coxen, Marshall Victoria Coxen		5 Mar. 1946

Case	Plaintiff	Defendant	Date
2957	Craft, Margaret L.		
		T. W. Craft	22 Apr. 1946
3196	Craft, Margaret L.		
		T. W. Craft	6 Nov. 1947
87214a	Craft, Rebecca Lynn		
		Daniel Richard Craft	16 Mar. 1988
4862	Craig, Geraldine Keith		
		William James Craig	7 June 1960
1702	Craig, H. D.		
		Erma Craig	28 Mar. 1933
6287	Craig, Karen Kaye		
		William Harry Craig	16 Feb. 1970
5631	Craig, Robert I. Sr.		
		Lillina L. Sullivan	11 Feb. 1966
7045	Cranfill, Stanley Wayne Key		
		Cheryl Cranfill	3 Aug. 1978
2711	Cravens, Dora		
		Thomas E. Cravens	9 Sept. 1944
2799	Crawford, Frankie L.		
		T. A. Crawford Jr.	25 May 1945
1927	Crawford, Mrs. M. L.		
		L. S. Crawford	26 Apr. 1935
2855	Crawford, S. A.		
		Helen Crawford	4 Sept. 1945
6033	Crenshaw, Dobie Faye		
		Jack Crenshaw	17 Sept. 1968
81178a	Crenshaw, Donna Brewton		
		Paul Anthony Crenshaw	4 Nov. 1981
4520	Crenshaw, Ellie		
		Fowler Crenshaw	16 Sept. 1957
5554	Crenshaw, Ellie Cobb		
		Fowler Crenshaw	6 Nov. 1965
3322	Crenshaw, Fowler		
		Nadine Crenshaw	22 Nov. 1948
5354	Crenshaw, Gloria Jean		
		Harry Vernon Crenshaw	31 Aug. 1964
6065	Crenshaw, John V.		
		Bessie A. Crenshaw	17 June 1968
4710	Crenshaw, Marvin A.		
		Allie Frances Crenshaw	19 May 1960
5807	Crenshaw, Marvin A. Jr.		
		Alice Emma Crenshaw	16 Feb. 1967
4620	Crenwelge, Anita L.		
		Nathaniel S. Crenwelge	21 July 1958

Case	Plaintiff	Defendant	Date
85114a	Crenwelge, Janice Jung		
		Brain Crenwelge	16 Aug. 1985
4414	Crider, A. Frances		
		Claud Crider	1 Apr. 1957
85186a	Crider, Carla Jean Yoeman		
		Rudy Lee Crider	8 Nov. 1985
3008	Crider, Ethel M.		
		Edward Crider	22 Aug. 1946
2894	Crider, James A.		
		Agnes V. Crider	25 Feb. 1946
4195	Crider, Lila Fay		
		Eugene Crider	11 May 1955
4983	Crider, Louise		
		Clarence D. Crider	25 Apr. 1962
86218a	Crider, Shirley A.		
		James R. Crider	19 Nov. 1986
7840a	Crider, Shirley Ann		
		James Robert Crider	10 Oct. 1978
5488	Crider, Maye Elizabeth		
		Eugene G. Crider	30 Apr. 1965
4528	Crider, Viola Lee		
		Arthur Norris Crider	26 Mar. 1959
8136a	Crocker, Nancy Jane		
		Howard L. Crocker	6 Apr. 1981
3272	Croom, Herbert		
		Lillian Croom	7 Sept. 1948
6280	Croom, Mildred Eddins		
		Joe B. Croom	29 Aug. 1969
2218	Crosby, Lillian		
		Carl C. Crosby	20 Sept. 1938
2961	Cross, Vernon		
		Ruby Lee Cross	22 Apr. 1946
3173	Cross, Vernon		
		Henrietta Cross	6 Nov. 1947
84119a	Crouch, Pamela Denice		
		Russell Lavelle Crouch	12 July 1984
3473	Crow, Annie M.		
		P. C. Crow	12 Dec. 1949
2946	Cullom, John H.		
		Dorothy Lee Cullom	22 Apr. 1946
2747	Culwell, Billie Lou		
		Thos. H. Culwell	25 Sept. 1944
1908	Culwell, Pauline		
		Homer Culwell	5 Apr. 1935

Case	Plaintiff	Defendant	Date
2911	Cummings, Lucille		
		John T. Cummings	25 Feb. 1946
2207	Cunningham, Annie M.		
		Geo. R. Cunningham	20 Sept. 1938
8256a	Cunningham, Elaine Katherine		
		Jack Lewis Cunningham	19 Apr. 1983
5908	Cunningham, James L.		
		Deloris L. Cunningham	8 Aug. 1967
8325a	Curbow, Claudia Nina		
		Alden Eugene Curbow	28 Sept. 1984
5957	Curlee, Johnnie Kathleen		
		James David Curlee	6 Oct. 1967
1793	Curry, Dawson		
		Susie Lee Curry	10 Oct. 1933
5223	Curry, Lula		
		John Floyd Curry	17 July 1963
7898a	Curtis, Kathy Antoinette		
		George Earl Curtis	23 Apr. 1980

D

Case	Plaintiff	Defendant	Date
2113	Dahl, Julius T.		
		Christine Dahl	19 Apr. 1937
84274a	Dale, George		
		Sylvia J. Dale	27 Dec. 1984
3511	Daly, Jno. S. Jr.		
		Grace J. Daly	26 June 1950
3065	Dambach, Jno. I.		
		Beulah D. Dambach	2 Jan. 1947
85269a	Daniel, Misty Lynn		
		Wallace Vernon Daniel	19 Dec. 1985
7972a	Daniels, Eugene		
		Altomease Daniels	21 Mar. 1980
4683	Daniels, Lillie R.		
		Barney E. Daniels	14 Jan. 1959
3022	Dantzler, Hy (Henry) R.		
		Mose Dantzler	25 Oct. 1946
2610	Dantzler, Ozler		
		Novella Dantzler	9 Oct. 1942
4149	Danuser, Lorraine C.		
		Norman K, Danuser	13 Dec. 1954
5565	Danz, Lillian Oleta		
		Leroy Milton Danz	8 Oct. 1965

Case	Plaintiff	Defendant	Date
3393	Darden, Ed Richard		
		Birdie M. Darden	28 Nov. 1950
85317a	Darnell, Betty T.		
		Robert J. Darnell	13 Feb. 1986
4222	Darr, Marion E.		
		Susie Lee Darr	12 Aug. 1955
2326	Davenport, Lois R.		
		Edward E. Davenport	19 Sept. 1939
4953	Davenport, Ruby		
		William George Davenport	8 June 1962
4499	Daves, Marie		
		Gordon Daves	21 June 1957
4587	Daves, Marie		
		Gordon Daves	19 June 1958
2982	Davidson, Rose Ellen		
		Max M. Davidson	3 Sept. 1946
4245	Davila, Dominga		
		Manuel Davila	5 Sept. 1955
3687	Davila, Madaline		
		Ygnacio Davila	5 Sept. 1951
82248a	Davis, Donald Lee		
		Liticia Davis	21 Jan. 1983
5457	Davis, Elsa		
		George W. Davis	14 Jan. 1965
4500	Davis, George		
		Mary Davis	26 Aug. 1957
1842	Davis, H. I.		
		Linnie Davis	27 Mar. 1934
5740	Davis, Herbert		
		Diane Kay Davis	7 Oct. 1966
80105a	Davis, Ida Mae		
		Timothy Cornell Davis	1 Dec. 1980
5991	Davis, Ila Jean		
		Victor Davis	26 June 1968
8319a	Davis, Lester R.		
		Chong Ye Davis	21 Apr. 1983
4442	Davis, Minnie H.		
		Ford Davis	29 Apr. 1957
5789	David, Oma Ruth		
		Clifton Herbert Davis	9 Dec. 1966
2531	Davis, Opal		
		W. A. Davis	6 Mar. 1942
3443	Davis, Pearl S.		
		E. T. Davis	13 Dec. 1949

Case	Plaintiff	Defendant	Date
2441	Davis, Roland		
		Lorene Davis	17 Sept. 1940
3221	Dawson, Hazel		
		Floyd C. Dawson	11 Sept. 1948
4081	Dawson, W. F.		
		Laura Dawson	26 July 1954
85220a	Day, Brenda		
		Anthony Lynn Day	4 Feb. 1986
2580	Day, Dorothy		
		Everett B. Day	17 Apr. 1942
5507	Day, Mary Lucy		
		Shelby H. Day	7 June 1965
4055	Dayton, Shirley		
		Ballard Edward Dayton	14 May 1954
5137	Dean, Ima Garrett		
		Weldon C. Dean	16 Jan. 1963
5336	Dearing, Mark Dock		
		Louise Freida Dearing	4 June 1964
1808	De Bellevue, Marceline F.		
		Clifton B. De Bellevue	25 Oct. 1933
8247a	Decker, Cinthia Johnson		
		David Ralph Decker	8 Oct. 1982
2442	Deering, L. R.		
		Zuma Goff Deering	1 Nov. 1940
3119	Deering, Oma Lee		
		Mark F. Deering	12 June 1947
4968	Deese, Ella Lee		
		Oscar R. Deese	20 May 1961
4159	Degado, Mary		
		Natividad Degado	12 Aug. 1955
2750	De La Cruz, Gertrudez		
		Alecia De La Cruz	5 Apr. 1945
84126a	DeLa Santos, Estella V.		
		Henry L. DeLa Santos	20 Dec. 1984
6860	Dela Santos, Henry Lara		
		Felcitas Dominguez	7 July 1977
3058	De Laune, L. A.		
		Jewel I. De Laune	2 Jan. 1947
79135a	Delgadillo, Guadulupe M.		
		James M. Delgadillo	6 Nov. 1979
86248a	Delgadillo, Jesse Frank		
		Shannon Kelly Hughes Delgadillo	
			18 Mar. 1987

Case	Plaintiff	Defendant	Date
6327	Delgadillo, Margaret	Joe Rodriguez Delgadillo	10 Jan. 1972
3931	Delgadillo, Mary	Charlie Delgadillo	22 Apr. 1953
85241a	Delgadillo, Rosemary J.	Jesse M. Delgadillo	19 Dec. 1985
5724	Delgado, Donna Lee	Arturo Jose Delgado	8 Aug. 1966
5823	Dell, Cynthia Jean	James Erik Dell	13 Feb. 1967
6418	DeLos Santos, Henry Lara	Esmeralda G. De Los Santos	30 Mar. 1971
2136	De Masters, Roxie	F. I. De Masters	30 Mar. 1937
2041	Demerritt, Ollie	Georcia Demerritt	16 Oct. 1936
86152a	Denny, Bruce Donald	Cathy Ann Denny	5 Oct. 1988
1889	Denton, B. F.	Louisiana S. Denton	5 Apr. 1935
6445	Denton, Vera Marie	Harry Ernest Denton	24 June 1970
3982	DeRosier, Lola G.	Edward Geo. DeRosier	11 Sept. 1953
81251a	Devlin, Pepper Elvira	Mark Anthony Devlin	30 Mar. 1982
4597	Devore, Anna Marie	Carl Eugene Devore	26 May 1958
5983	Diaz, Nancy S.	David Diaz	21 June 1968
5090	Dickens, Margaret	Joseph Howard Dickens	12 Mar. 1962
6425	Dickerson, Arthur P	Rosalind D. Dickerson	28 May 1970
81120a	Dickerson, Diana Gayle	Gary Ewell Dicker son	20 Oct. 1981
2779	Diddens, Herman E.	Bathelle Diddens	25 May 1945
3090	Dietert, Alma D.	Albert R. Dietert	15 Feb. 1947
2574	Dietert, Lonie	R. C. Dietert	19 Dec. 1944

Case	Plaintiff	Defendant	Date
2541	Difer, Sidney C.		
		Lucille Difer	29 Sept. 1941
867a	Diggs, Ellen Raso		
		Chas. Carroll Diggs	24 Mar. 1986
4175	Dimery, George L.		
		Rosa Dimery	21 Feb. 1956
4428	Dimery, Helen		
		John Dimery	28 May 1958
2411	Dimery, Janie		
		William Dimery	28 Oct. 1940
4711	Dintleman, G. F.		
		Margaret Dintleman	31 Mar. 1959
1636	Dinwiddie, G. F.		
		Ada Dinwiddie	6 Oct. 1931
4495	Diss, James H.		
		Mellie H. Diss	9 Sept, 1957
5693	Dixon, David		
		Maggie Bell Dixon	21 Sept. 1966
2731	Dixon, David E.		
		Gwendolyn Dixon	5 Sept. 1944
3857	Dixon, E. David		
		Georgia Mae Dixon	15 Dec. 1952
3887	Dixon, Frances Nell		
		Ollie Lecil Dixon Jr.	2 Feb. 1953
3968	Dixon, Jo Ann		
		Ollie Lecil Dixon	17 July 1953
3037	Dixon, Joseph I.		
		Flora J. Dixon	25 Oct. 1946
70173a	Dodd, Corky Lee		
		Anita N. Dodd	3 Nov. 1981
85187a	Dominguez, Elaina Sandoval		
		Joaquin Mendez Dominguez	24 Apr. 1986
8292a	Dominguez, Esmeralda R.		
		Romaon G. Dominguez	30 Aug. 1982
8562a	Donaldson, David Alan		
		Linda Jean Donaldson	25 June 1985
80260a	Donihoo, Eleanor Louise		
		Danny Lynn Donihoo	13 Mar. 1981
4821	Donohoe, Harry G.		
		Marie Teresa Donohoe	3 Oct. 1960
3535	Dorado, Jesus		
		Antonia Dorado	25 Sept. 1950
5948	Dorsett, Altha		
		Scott Owen Dorsett	25 Oct. 1967

Case	Plaintiff	Defendant	Date
6819	Doty, Nannie D. Adair	Cecil Edward Doty	? Apr. 1977
8192a	Doty, Rosemary Faire	John Martin Doty	16 June 1981
5325	Douglas, Goldie	Richard H. Douglas	17 Apr. 1964
4841	Douglas, Henrietta	Melvin Douglas	17 Dec, 1963
3492	Doughty, Paul C.	Ora T. Doughty	19 Apr. 1950
2646	Dover, Lorraine	O'Neil Dover	24 May 1943
2820	Dowd, Queen	Milo T. Doowd	14 Sept. 1945
2317	Dowdy, Alfa M.	James Dowdy	30 Mar. 1939
3924	Downum, Eunice M.	Kenneth B. Downum	13 Apr. 1953
79182a	Dozier, James Michael	Danita Reeves	21 Nov. 1979
8520a	Dragoo, Geneva Chadwick	Allen Crawford Dragoo	24 Apr. 1985
7057	Dreibrodt, Cynthia Ann	Patrick Claude Dreibrodt	13 Oct. 1980
4339	Duckworth, Claudia	Robert Duckworth	10 July 1956
5041	Duckworth, Joyce Virginia	Emmett Wilson Duckworth	30 Oct. 1961
5570	Duckworth, Mary Esther	Donald Duckworth	20 Nov. 1965
6235	Duckworth, Rosenda S.	Donald E. Duckworth	24 Aug. 1970
5267	Duckworth, Sandra S.	Ronald E. Duckworth	16 Oct. 1963
2421	Duddleston, Marie	Roy Duddleston	18 Sept. 1940
2438	Duderstadt, Sybil	Fred Duderstadt	17 Sept. 1940
88100a	Dukes, Jackie N.	Shirley Ann Sheharn Dukes	5 July 1988
4285	Dumphy, Jack L.	Lois A. Dumphy	20 Dec. 1955

Case	Plaintiff	Defendant	Date
4364	Duncan, Mary J.		
		Chester A. Duncan	6 Aug. 1956
4524	Duncan, Robert W.		
		Grace L. Duncan	3 Mar. 1958
8594a	Dunn, Kathleen Ann		
		Bobby D. Dunn	25 June 1985
5722	Duran, Elisa		
		Gener Duran	8 Aug. 1968
81115a	Durna, Elizabeth J.		
		Fernando Duran	10 Sept. 1980
5243	Durbon, Doris M.		
		Carson Durbon	9 Aug. 1963
2732	Durst, George William		
		Claudia J. Durst	6 Sept. 1944
3406	Dwyer, Alta Lee		
		William S. Dwyer	18 July 1949
5802	Dyer, Shirley Faye		
		Gerry Windel Dyer	20 Feb. 1967
2727	Dyson, Lela Mae		
		Joseph Roy Dyson	9 June 1944

E

Case	Plaintiff	Defendant	Date
6120	Eaglebarger, Danette		
		Gene Eaglebarger	9 May 1969
4557	Eaglebarger, H. E.		
		Marilyn Eaglebarger	7 Feb. 1958
7864a	Eaglebarger, Howard E.		
		Sandra Kay Eaglebarger	31 Oct. 1978
4378	Eary, Irene Johnson		
		Joe Henry Eary	17 Sept. 1956
2205	Eason, Katherine		
		Thurmon D.Eason	20 Sept. 1938
3167	Easter, Anthony		
		Margie Easter	3 Sept. 1947
3579	Eathorne, Anne O'Pearl		
		Frank G. Eathorne	2 Nov. 1950
1614	Ebert, Henry		
		Teresa Ebert	22 Apr. 1931
3602	Eckhardt, Doris		
		Milton Eckhardt	13 Sept. 1951
88138a	Eckstein, Patricia Yvette		
		Robert Louis Eckstein	22 Aug. 1988

Case	Plaintiff	Defendant	Date
2137	Eckstein, Walter		
		Anna R. Eckstein	22 Sept. 1937
2307	Eckstein, Walter		
		Anna R. Eckstein	28 Mar. 1939
2856	Edmonds, Henry		
		June Lee Edmonds	6 Sept. 1943
2969	Edmonds, Henry		
		June Edmonds	5 June 1946
4210	Edmonds, Henry		
		Lucille C. Edmonds	12 Aug. 1955
4163	Edmonds, Wanda June		
		Jerry K. Edmonds	9 Nov. 1955
2615	Edmondson, E. Mildred		
		E. B. Edmondson	15 Mar. 1943
3219	Edmundson, E. B.		
		Wilda Edmundson	2 Feb. 1948
3367	Edmundson, E. B.		
		Wilda Edmundson	14 Mar. 1949
4442	Edmundson, Eugene B.		
		Melba Lee Edmundson	9 Apr. 1957
3541	Edwards, Amelia		
		Jack Edwards	25 Sept, 1950
79120a	Edwards, Arthur Ray		
		Barbara Edwards	20 Dec. 1979
3668	Edwards, Betty Jo		
		Harry H. Edwards	4 Sept. 1951
5161	Edwards, Catherine		
		James W. Edwards	9 Jan. 1963
4415	Edwards, Edna		
		James W. Edwards	4 Mar. 1957
2905	Edwards, Edwin		
		Louise Edwards	25 Feb. 1946
837a	Edwards, Kimberly Jo		
		Jesse Raymond Edwards	16 Jan. 1984
3153	Edwards, Lola		
		Leo H. Edwards	7 Aug. 1947
3514	Edwards, Louis		
		Billie B. Edwards	19 May 1950
3662	Edwards, Lucille		
		Jack Edwards	18 June 1951
4393	Eggers, Dorothy Gwendolyn		
		Ernest Wm. Eggers	17 Oct. 1956
4618	Eggers, Alice		
		Ernest Eggers	10 July 1959

Case	Plaintiff	Defendant	Date
1943	Eggleston, Joseph B.		
		Annie Eggleston	8 Oct. 1938
4745	Elam, Florence		
		Kelly Elam	2 June 1959
5298	Elam, Vera C.		
		Kelly L. Elam	9 May 1964
3294	Eldridge, Lewis W. Jr.		
		Lucile S. Eldridge	8 Sept. 1948
6810	Elie, Zenobia L.		
		Johnnie Alfred Elie	7 Apr. 1977
6981	Ellebracht, Edna Marie		
		Ellis Edgar Ellebracht	5 Jan. 1978
85219a	Ellington, Randace A.		
		Carrie Lynn Ellington	21 Oct. 1985
5931	Elliott, Josephine N.		
		Leonard Gray Elliott	13 Oct. 1967
5065	Ellis, Daisy Inez		
		Buck Elton Evans	8 Jan. 1962
3957	Ellis, Marjorie		
		Joseph Guy Ellis	13 July 1953
3352	Emsley, W. R.		
		Minnie Emsley	2 Feb. 1949
81218a	England, Christine Lee Smith		
		Nick Louis England	5 Jan. 1982
82169a	England, Janet L.		
		Jack E. England	5 Nov. 1982
8811a	England, Raylene M.		
		Tyrone C. England	5 May 1988
4241	Englehardt, H. C.		
		Joyce Englehardt	5 Sept. 1955
2806	Engleman, Hugh B.		
		Gladys B. Engleman	25 May 1945
2870	Engleman, Theresa F.		
		Hugh B. Engleman Jr.	13 Nov. 1945
1904	Ensley, Samanthy		
		Ed Easley	19 Apr. 1935
2175	Epple, Neal		
		George L. Epple	30 Nov. 1937
85314a	Ericson, Deborah Jeanine		
		William R. Ericson	14 Nov. 1986
85120a	Ernst, Michelle Diane		
		Michael Jay Evans	31 July 1985

Case	Plaintiff / Defendant	Date
5132	Erwin, William Thomas	
	Myrtle Frances Sewaller Erwin	30 Aug. 1962
2477	Espinosa, John	
	Santos Espinosa	29 Sept. 1941
3168	Espinosa, Jose M.	
	Lilly Espinosa	28 July 1947
3025	Espinosa, Julia	
	Manuel Espinosa	3 Feb. 1947
1577	Espinosa, Selia	
	Seferino Espinosa	23 Mar. 1932
1592	Espinosa, Selia	
	Seferino Espinosa	19 Apr. 1932
2158	Espinosa, Zorogosa	
	L. C. Espinosa	29 Sept. 1937
1736	Espinoza, Seferino	
	Selia Espinoza	11 Oct. 1934
3257	Esquedo, Joe R.	
	Nellie Esquedo	14 June 1948
3463	Estes, Mary Louise	
	Ned B. Estes Jr.	14 Nov. 1949
84111a	Evans, Cleo Mae	
	Ronald Wesley Evans	21 June 1984
85218a	Evans, Debbie Lynn	
	Chas. Richard Evans	23 Apr. 1986
2471	Evans, Dorothy	
	Horace Evans	11 Mar. 1941
4882	Evans, Dorothy	
	James Robt. Evans	27 July 1960
85236a	Evans, Gail Hubble	
	Jesse Evans	8 Nov. 1985
8893a	Evans, Judy Lee	
	Robert T. Evans	5 July 1988
79163a	Evans, Kathy Lynn	
	Ronald Wesley Evans	23 Jan. 1981
4308	Evans, Maxine E.	
	Vance E. Evans	9 Apr. 1956
83139a	Evans, Pricilla Marie	
	Michael Jay Evans	31 July 1985
3606	Everage, Lydia	
	Odell Everage	29 Jan. 1951

Case	Plaintiff	Defendant	Date
2023	Fairbanks, Annie		
		Robert Fairbnks	21 Apr. 1936
3197	Faircloth, Marie		
		Captain Faircloth	15 Dec. 1947
4298	Fare, Bennie		
		Janie Fare	7 May 1956
2572	Farmer, Eunice D.		
		George C. Farmer	10 Mar. 1942
5318	Farmer, Ruby L.		
		James W. Farmer	2 Apr. 1964
833a	Farr, Alvin		
		Sheila L. Farr	7 Apr. 1983
6009	Farr, Minnie Mae		
		Calvin Farr	13 Feb. 1968
3631	Farrar, Ethel		
		Carlon C. Farrar	23 Apr. 1951
86184a	Farrington, Harrison Mc Dale		
		Jean Ann Farrington	19 Sept. 1986
8366a	Farris, Mary Janette		
		Wm. Jessie Farris	15 Sept. 1983
87135a	Farish, Judy R.		
		Michael E. Farish	31 Aug. 1987
8082a	Farshabi, Kansliz(?) T.		
		Rose Farshani	18 July 1980
85233a	Faulkner, Ward Jack		
		Malane Glaze Faulkner	2 Nov. 1985
87123a	Faure, Rita C.		
		Robert C. Faure	16 Sept. 1987
2895	Fawcett, Scott		
		Grace Fawcett	2 Jan. 1945
81196a	Fees, Wilma Frances		
		Harold W. Fees	21 Dec. 1981
4373	Felix, Mary Sue		
		Willie Fern Felix	19 Oct. 1956
1759	Fellows, Ada		
		Jno. A. Fellows	28 Mar. 1933
3204	Fellay, Bobbie Lee		
		Blair Fellay	15 Dec. 1947
5943	Ferguson, Arden Ann		
		Franklin Ferguson Jr.	3 Jan. 1968
1878	Ferguson, Connie		
		Earl Ferguson	9 Oct. 1934
5074	Ferguson, Dorothy		
		David C. Ferguson	29 Jan. 1962

Case	Plaintiff	Defendant	Date
1882	Ferguson, Lettie Leona		
		David F. Ferguson	17 Oct. 1934
4447	Fernandez, Ervey Jesse		
		Mary Ellen Fernandez	2 Apr. 1957
7856a	Fiedler, Elsie A.		
		Kermit A. Fiedler	13 Dec. 1979
83209a	Fife, Claudie		
		Benjamin F. Fife	4 Jan. 1984
3632	Fifer, Lester G.		
		Willie Rae Fifer	10 Sept. 1951
6179	Fifer, Mary		
		Allen Fifer	17 Mar. 1969
1656	Fikes, Gladys		
		Lloyd Fikes	12 Oct. 1931
2771	Fikes, Mildred F.		
		Homer Fikes	8 Feb. 1945
5236	Filbeck, Lettie		
		Raymond Filbeck	11 May 1964
87188a	Findley, Deborah J.		
		Lawrence F. Findley	24 May 1989
3003	Fine, Jewell		
		Dozier Lee Fine	22 July 1946
4984	Finn, Dorothy		
		John Finn	5 June 1961
8371a	Fischer, Pricilla Rodriguez		
		Michael Lee Fischer	25 May 1983
79111a	Fisher, Annie I.		
		Jerry Wayne Fisher	26 Feb. 1980
808a	Fisher, Robert W.		
		Wanda Joyce Fisher	16 Jan. 1981
8079a	Fisher, Sherry Matthews		
		John C. Fisher	12 June 1980
8787a	Fitzgerald, Marcia Jennifer		
		Harold E. Fitzgerald Jr.	24 June 1987
86107a	Flaherty, Kelley Morgan		
		Michael Flaherty Jr.	21 Nov. 1986
86268a	Fleming, Norma Lee		
		James A. Fleming	22 Apr. 1987
2074	Flenninkin, Met. L.		
		Addie A. Flenninkin	19 Oct. 1936
2111	Flenninkin, Cecil		
		W. M. Flenninkin	19 Apr. 1937
6105	Flick, Sharon Lynn		
		Timothy M. Flick	14 July 1969

Case	Plaintiff	Defendant	Date
81226a	Flora, Jimmie Jean		
		Thomas Dean Flora	7 Jan. 1982
1578	Flores, Caterine		
		Florinda Flores	31 Mar. 1931
5977	Flores, Sylvia J.		
		Richard A. Flores	17 Mar. 1969
8137a	Flournoy, Kathleen Bartell		
		Kenoth H. Flournoy	12 June 1981
4559	Flowers, Amelie		
		Elester Flowers	19 May 1958
3786	Fluitt, Holly Fay		
		Edward N. Fluitt	25 Apr. 1952
2539	Fluitt, Lonnie B.		
		Lillian F. Fluitt	10 Mar. 1942
3399	Fluitt, Mabel		
		Nelson Fluitt	23 May 1949
5698	Fogle, Helen		
		Reed Fogle	20 Apr. 19667
5435	Ford, Helen		
		Clarence Ford	28 June 1965
1790	Ford, Mrs. Willie		
		Elgin Ford	10 Oct. 1933
6945	Foreman, Ann		
		James E. Foreman	23 Nov. 1977
2714	Forgy, Eunice		
		T. L. Forgy	9 June 1944
82278a	Forrester, Julie Bess		
		George Thomas Forrester	14 Oct. 1983
86149a	Fortner, Thomas D.		
		Helen Jo Fortner	21 Oct. 1987
83103a	Fossler, Rebecca Eliz.		
		Douglas Earl Fossler	12 July 1983
2011	Foster, Jimmie		
		Charles Foster	23 Apr. 1936
4803	Foster, Joe Nell		
		Jimmie Douglas Foster	17 Aug. 1960
6099	Fowler, Lola		
		Charles S. Fowler	16 Dec. 1968
85130a	Fowler, Peggy		
		Eura Fowler	20 Sept. 1985
84328a	Fox, Elsie Marie		
		Edward James Fox	28 Mar. 1984
2776	Fox, Hazel		
		Lee Fox	18 Jan. 1945

Case	Plaintiff	Defendant	Date
3411	Fox, Hazel		
	Lee S. Fox		18 Aug. 1949
3158	Fox, Hazel C.		
	Lee S. Fox		5 Aug. 1947
80194a	Fralichs, Delores Mae		
	Jemmy Don Fralichs		17 Nov. 1980
2665	Francis, Tappan E.		
	Anna E. Francis		6 Dec. 1943
6385	Frank, Doris Sue		
	Richard A. Frank		21 May 1970
5801	Frank, Ronald D.		
	Annie E. Frank		17 Jan 1967
2875	Franks, Mary E.		
	George T. Franks		13 Nov. 1945
3955	Franks, Mary Elizabeth		
	George T. Franks		16 July 1953
3967	Frazier, Pansy Rae		
	Burton D. Frazier		26 Oct. 1953
4023	Frederick, Wilburn H.		
	Virginia Lee Frederick		7 Dec. 1953
8560a	Freeman, Donna Lynn		
	Donald Freeman		23 May 1985
2424	Freeman, J. W.		
	Mamie Freeman		18 Sept. 1940
2435	Freeman, Jane T.		
	Jim G. Freeman		18 Sept. 1940
2974	Freeman, W. P.		
	Elizabeth Freeman		5 June 1946
81123a	Frincke, Louise W.		
	Martin C. Frincke		6 Aug. 1981
3714	Fritz, Felix Joseph		
	Gussie Forman R. Fritz		19 Oct. 1951
6407	Fritz, Gerald		
	Lowanna W. Fritz		5 May 1970
2208	Frost, John		
	Callie Frost		3 Sept. 1938
1744	Frost, Sallie		
	Jon Frost		20 Oct. 1932
821a	Fry, Rod		
	Tina Fry		28 May 1982
79232a	Fry, Vera Louise		
	David Lloyd Fry		26 Feb. 1980
4720	Fuel, Luther		
	Ernestine P. Fuel		13 Mar. 1959

Case	Plaintiff	Defendant	Date
6288	Fugier, Robert Edward		
	Linda Kay Fugier		2 Sept. 1969
8579a	Fulk, Marc Skilon		
	Keely Sue Fulk		28 Aug. 1985
86189a	Fulk, Marc		
	Michelle Stokes Fulk		24 Apr. 1987
3441	Fuller, Katherine W.		
	Gordon A. Fuller		12 Dec. 1949
4743	Fuller, Mary Jane		
	Troy E. Fuller		1 June 1959
1667	Fuller, Nell Frances		
	Hurley E. Fuller		21 Oct. 1931
4851	Fullick, Jacksie B.		
	Thomas E. Fullick		19 Apr. 1960
79208a	Furman, Janice Cowan		
	Philip Huey Furman		6 Mar. 1980
84316a	Fusco, Christy C.		
	Guy J. Fusco		24 Jan 1985

G

Case	Plaintiff	Defendant	Date
8543a	Gafford, Norma Hughes		
	David Wayne Gafford		8 May 1985
215	Gage, Sarah C.		
	John D. Gage		?? Nov. 1887
5294	Gallavis, Louis Jr.		
	Mary Lee Gallavis		7 Jan. 1964
5984	Galoway, Billie Jean		
	Harmon Ned Galloway		13 Feb. 1968
5808	Garcia, Amado		
	Andrea Garcia		16 Jan. 1967
5280	Garcia, Ernest		
	Nancy Garcia		29 Feb. 1964
2869	Garcia, Esperanza		
	Exiquis Garcia		22 Apr. 1945
2618	Garcia, Genero		
	Carolina Garcia		16 Mar. 1943
1883	Garcia, Marceana		
	Enijo Garcia		13 Oct. 1934
79225a	Garcia, Maria Frausto		
	Imoconcio Garcia		7 May 1980
86148a	Garcia, Rebecca Ann		
	Hector Garcia		28 July 1986

44

Case	Plaintiff	Defendant	Date
2393	Gardner, Annie M. Leland E. Gardner		19 Mar. 1940
3150	Gardner, Billie Adolph Gardner		5 Aug. 1947
3174	Gardner, Ida Rose Joe R. Gardner		6 Nov. 1947
2221	Gardner, Leland E. Eula Marie Gardner		20 Sept. 1938
3657	Gardner, Leonora Stanley L. Gardner		18 May 1951
80172a	Gardner, Linda Ann Webb Roy Norman Gardner		31 Oct. 1980
2042	Garrett, Koreske Chester Garrett		21 Oct. 1936
2849	Garrett, Lillian Gordon Garrett		5 Sept. 1945
2018	Garrett, Mary Jimmie L. Garrett		14 Apr. 1936
3205	Garrett, Warren Jr. Frankie Garrett		15 Dec. 1947
3966	Gary, Leona Besier Jack Gary		13 June 1953
3647	Gary, Melba Lee Vernon M. Gary		24 Apr. 1951
3218	Garza, Alvino Elvira Garza		3 Feb. 1948
5573	Garza, Edward Marines Mary Martinez Garza		3 Mar. 1966
83305a	Garza, Ernest Ayala Rosa Amparo Garza		8 Mar. 1984
2980	Garza, Josephine T. Alvino Garza		5 June 1946
5869	Garza, Margarita Richard Garza		5 June 1967
84100a	Gass, Monica L. Timothy R. Gass		21 June 1984
3518	Gates, Julia Hy. H. Gates		26 June 1950
3033	Gates, Olive Pearl Robert E. Gates		6 Sept. 1946
3568	Gathings, Dorothy J. Paul E. Gathings		17 Nov. 1950
4762	Gattis, Irene Ernest Gattis		27 Oct. 1959

45

Case	Plaintiff	Defendant	Date
5592	Geisen, Imogene		
		Sherman Geisen	4 Feb. 1966
85152a	Gelbolinga, Bellie		
		Gideon Gelbolinga	12 Sept. 1985
3222	Gentry, J. A.		
		Willie Ava Gentry	11 Aug. 1948
4388	George, Joseph T.		
		Loretta George	19 Oct. 1957
5431	George, Molly		
		Thomas George	13 Jan. 1965
3131	George, Naomi		
		Eugene E. George	10 June 1947
2755	Gibson, john A.		
		Louise M. Gibson	19 Dec. 1944
1757	Gibson, Silvas		
		Theoria Gibson	29 Mar. 1933
2844	Gibson, Silvan L.		
		Irene Gibson	8 Oct. 1945
80102a	Gilbert, Janice		
		Nila Gilbert	30 July 1980
3645	Gill, Robert S.		
		Cleo Jennie Gill	24 Apr. 1951
2054	Gillerman, Lena		
		Herbert Gillerman	7 Oct. 1936
4295	Gilmore, Mary		
		Ovide Lee Gilmore	7 May 1956
3856	Ginter, Margie Jo		
		Stanely Ginter	15 Dec. 1952
5387	Gipson, Christine Graham		
		Harold E. Gipson	3 Sept. 1964
5617	Gipson, Juanetta A.		
		Harold E. Gipson	18 Jan. 1966
84297a	Girard, Perry Faye		
		Ronald Lee Girard	25 June 1985
88103a	Glaze, Frances Eugenia		
		Robert R. Glaze	8 Dec. 1988
2709	Glenn, Lillie		
		R. C. Glenn	27 Mar. 1944
3237	Glenn, Sam		
		Lorene Glenn	25 Oct. 1948
3148	Glosson, Alma		
		James E. Glosson	5 Mar. 1948
3072	Glover, Hazel		
		Vance S. Glover	2 Jan. 1947

Case	Plaintiff	Defendant	Date
5655	Glover, Virginia		
		Howard Jodie Glover	23 June 1966
4746	Godwin, Wilma Dean Mayo		
		Harlan Hart Godwin	10 June 1989
81109a	Goette, Janet Rae Whitaker		
		Michael Earl Goette	30 July 1981
6248	Goff, Annie Yokley		
		Lee Goff	14 July 1969
5816	Goff, Dolores		
		Dorman Goff	30 Mar. 1967
6029	Goff, Dorman		
		Rachel Goff	20 Sept. 1968
2463	Goff, Mary		
		V. B. Goff	25 Mar. 1941
4467	Goff, Myrtle Eva		
		Henry Clay Goff	20 Mar. 1957
1952	Goff, Ruby		
		L. D. Goff	12 Oct. 1935
6064	Going, Helen S.		
		Chas E. Going Jr.	15 July 1968
79168a	Gold, Jackie Don		
		Nancy Lee Gold	29 Oct. 1979
3890	Goldman, L. J.		
		Jackie Nola Goldman	15 Dec. 1952
2902	Goldman, Lila Lee		
		Jesse D. Goldman	25 Feb. 1946
87183a	Goldman, Marl		
		Marilyn Gail Goldman	6 Apr. 1988
4740	Gonzales, Andrea		
		Vincente Gonzales	6 May 1960
4317	Gonzales, Concepcion		
		Aundio Gonzales	10 Jan. 1957
4686	Gonzales, Delia		
		Candido Gonzales	20 June 1959
87278a	Gonzales, Diane Peralta		
		John Gonzales	8 Sept. 1988
2715	Gonzales, Jose		
		Concha Gonzales	18 May 1944
2487	Gonzales, Juan		
		Crencencia P. Gonzales	18 Sept. 1941
2661	Gonzales, Juan		
		Paula Gonzales	2 Aug. 1943
6007	Gonzales, Maria de Jesus Fabro		
		Tomas Vargas Gonzales	4 Mar. 1968

Case	Plaintiff	Defendant	Date
6488	Gonzales, Rogelio Jr.		
		Irma P. Gonzales	15 Jan. 1971
2551	Gonzales, Ruben		
		Dolores Gonzales	10 Mar. 1942
86319a	Gonzales, Terri Irene		
		James Dominguez Gonzales	18 Feb. 1987
1893	Gooch, Myry		
		Elvie Gooch	10 Oct. 1933
5719	Goodall Bobbie Sue		
		Felton R. Goodall	8 Aug. 1966
5073	Goodall, Felton Ray		
		Patsy Gene Gegion Goodall	
			21 Aug. 1962
86195a	Goodloe, Roderick F.		
		Sharon L. Goodloe	30 Sept. 1986
4181	Goodloe, Stella Magaline		
		Walter Wallace Goodloe	11 May 1955
6953	Goodman, Virgil Lavonne		
		Tom Edward Goodman	8 Dec. 1977
5306	Goodson, Janice Lynn		
		Jim Goodson	27 July 1964
4759	Gordon, Maggie M.		
		Allie Gordon	24 July 1959
8067a	Gordon, Wilma Gail		
		James Franklin Gordon	5 June 1980
2901	Gormon, Ruth M.		
		Ed. J. Gormon	25 Feb. 1946
82122a	Gorrell, Cecilia		
		Stanley Louis Gorrell	1 Sept. 1982
2043	Gose, Elizabeth		
		Paul R. Gose	9 Oct. 1936
4349	Goss, Donald		
		Barbara Jean Goss	14 Aug. 1956
2864	Goss, J. O.		
		Thelma Goss	5 Jan. 1945
4335	Goss, J. O.		
		Zula Goss	10 July 1956
5087	Goss, J. O.		
		Zula Goss	25 June 1962
3527	Goss, Maydell		
		Joe H. Goss	26 June 1950
3336	Gotthard, Annie		
		Wm. C. Gotthard	9 Feb. 1949

Case	Plaintiff	Defendant	Date
84329a	Gould, David Wayne		
		Cherlynn Dawn Gould	28 Aug. 1985
81147a	Gower, Clara Strong Phillips		
		Robert D. Gower	18 Sept. 1981
81105a	Grace, Lena Mae		
		Charles O. Grace	21 Aug. 1981
7841a	Grady, Bill Watkins		
		Shirley Bobbie Grady	9 Nov. 1978
5638	Grady, Shirley		
		B. W. Grady	18 Feb. 1966
5885	Graham, Ann Baker		
		Ray Lee Graham	7 June 1967
5311	Graham, Diana		
		Roy Lee Graham	29 June 1964
2835	Graham, Elihu		
		Mattie Graham	16 July 1945
6046	Graham, Helen Garner		
		Lee Roy Graham	8 July 1968
81231a	Graham, Idill Sutton		
		Gray Graham	19 Feb. 1982
2921	Graham, Lee R.		
		Betty L. Graham	25 Feb. 1946
2527	Graham, Orville		
		Christine Graham	27 Mar. 1942
4472	Graham, Orville W.		
		Mary Margaret Graham	7 June 1957
1760.5	Graham, Oscar		
		Helen Graham	8 Apr. 1933
8533a	Graham. Vivian Lavern		
		Robert Ezra Graham	18 Oct. 1985
3007	Grantham, Ben F.		
		Bernice E. Grantham	7 Nov. 1946
3805	Grasham, Inez Mary		
		Paul Grasham	12 Aug. 1952
2286	Graves, Jeptha		
		Myrtle Graves	7 Mar. 1939
2671	Graves, Willie Mae		
		W. J. Graves	16 Sept. 1943
6630	Gray, Dorothy Mae		
		Wallace Mitchell Gray	22 Apr. 1974
4084	Gray, Margaret L.		
		John R. Gray	26 July 1954

Case	Plaintiff	Defendant	Date
8296a	Gray, Mindy Lynnette		
		Ronald Scott Gray	16 Sept. 1982
7932a	Gray, Ruth M.		
		Robert Bruce Gray	8 Nov. 1979
5443	Grayson, James Monroe		
		Edith Henry Garyson	5 Jan. 1965
4879	Green, Ruth Evelyn		
		Harold Lloyd Griffin	15 Aug. 1950
8519a	Green, Wynona Gains		
		Daniel Miller Green	24 Sept. 1985
8389a	Greeno, Kimberly Ann		
		Bernard Ty Greeno	23 June 1983
2689	Greer, Jeannie		
		Stuart Greer	6 Dec. 1943
4916	Greeson, Barbara Joann		
		Kenneth C. Greeson	4 Jan. 1961
2954	Greeson, Clifton A.		
		Pauline Greeson	22 Apr. 1946
2508	Gregory, Beatrice		
		Thomas S. Gregory	12 July 1941
3906	Gregory, Lorene		
		William D. Gregory	22 Apr. 1953
1760	Grey, Leona		
		Henry Grey	4 Apr. 1933
80112a	Gribble, Peggy Sue		
		Gary Don Gribble	30 July 1980
7037	Grier, Brenda Fay		
		James Timothy Grier	28 Sept. 1978
1928	Griffin, Gladys		
		Clarence Griffin	23 Apr. 1934
4684	Griffin, Harvey		
		Florence Elizabeth Griffin	
			4 June 1959
4803	Griffin, Maureen		
		Lloyd Griffin	4 Jan. 1960
78113a	Griffin, Mikel E.		
		Mary Merino Griffin	3 Feb. 1979
6268	Griffin, Peggy		
		Vernon Edward Griffin	20 Apr. 1970
3436	Griffin, Ruby		
		S. L. Griffin	11 Oct. 1949
1731	Griffin, Walter M.		
		Lydia Bell Griffin	18 Oct. 1932

Case	Plaintiff	Defendant	Date
6207	Grindland, Estella O.		
		Leonard J. Grindland	8 May 1969
5976	Grindland, Leonard J.		
		Duk Cha Lee Grindland	29 Nov. 1967
85212a	Groff, Alice Eva Rose		
		Ernest Fred Groff III	11 Oct. 1985
6462	Grogg, Sherilyn		
		David V. J. Grogg	4 Dec. 1970
2800	Grollimund, Mattie Lee		
		Joe E. Grollimund	5 Apr. 1945
6187	Grona, Cherri Dianne		
		Charles M. Grona	13 Mar. 1969
3428	Grona, Herman R.		
		Virginia Lee Grona	11 Oct. 1949
3544	Grona, Herman R.		
		Virginia Lee Grona	24 Sept. 1951
85287a	Grona, Nani Isenberg		
		Richard Merlin Grona	20 Feb. 1986
80255a	Grona, Patsy Lorane		
		Richard C. Grona	13 May 1981
8233a	Gonzales, Pedro P.		
		Maria Alaya Gonzales	11 June 1982
4061	Gross, Margaret		
		Vernon Gross	14 May 1954
88236a	Gross, Orrin L.		
		Waunita J. B. Gross	21 Dec. 1988
3839	Gross, Ruby		
		A. L. Gross	22 Apr. 1953
3283	Gross, Vernon Tom		
		Ellie Gross	8 Sept. 1948
2334	Gryder, Louis		
		J. B. Gryder (Grider)	19 Sept. 1939
5793	Guana, Domingo		
		Concepeon Guana	27 Mar. 1967
81230a	Guerrero, Dianna D.		
		Pedro Dela Cruz Guerrero	5 Nov. 1982
3555	Guerrero, Ramero V.		
		Rosa A. Guerrero	1 Jan. 1951
4381	Guidry, Mary Lee		
		Cleveland Guidry	19 Oct. 1956
83107a	Guinn, Elaine Smith		
		David Lee Guinn	4 Sept. 1984
108	Gunn, John M.		
		Rebecca A. Gunn	18 Mar. 1881

Case	Plaintiff	Defendant	Date
8763a	Gunter, Kimberly Ann		
		Raymond Allen Gunter	10 June 1988
5180	Gunter, Nina S.		
		Ramsdell B. Gunter	14 Mar. 1963
2451	Gusman, Samuel		
		Amalia A. Gusman	17 Sept. 1940
4514	Guthrie, Irene		
		Lloyd Guthrie	30 Sept. 1957
2075	Gutierres, Ferdinand		
		Estervon Gutierres	17 Oct. 1936
2628	Gutierrez, Alejandro		
		Ruby S. Guiterrez	15 Mar. 1943
8220a	Guiterrez, Edith Marie		
		Gary Gene Guiterrez	12 July 1982
4157	Gutierrez, Ezekiel		
		Janie K. Guiterrez	22 Sept. 1955
5827	Guiterrez, Ezekiel		
		Ann Guiterrez	20 Apr. 1967
5078	Gutierrez, Joe		
		Mary Ann Gutierrez	5 June 1962
2891	Gutierrez, Ramon		
		Lily Gutierrez	2 Jan. 1946
4293	Gutierrez, Salvador R.		
		Mary Gutierrez	27 Mar. 1956
4313	Guzik, Navada		
		Stanley Guzik	4 June 1956

H

Case	Plaintiff	Defendant	Date
82167a	Haas, Russell Eugene		
		Linda Lee Haas	3 Feb. 1983
2346	Habecker, Emil		
		Viola Habecker	19 Sept. 1939
1771	Haby, Lottie Sardonia		
		Robert George Haby	14 Apr. 1933
861a	Hackney, Brenda Reven		
		Bruce Jordon Hackney	24 Mar. 1986
5857	Hadley, Anne Marcia		
		Robert Zeb Hadley	9 Sept. 1967
8831a	Hagan, James C.		
		Tommy Rene Hagan	15 Feb. 1989
4470	Hagerty, Kathryn Anita		
		Wm. Frank Hagerty	24 June 1957

Case	Plaintiff	Defendant	Date
2321	Hagerty, Myrtle		
		W. J. Hagerty	25 Apr. 1939
1949	Hahn, W. E. (Bill)		
		Marion Hahn	15 Oct. 1935
8743a	Hale, James Cecil		
		Crystaline Denae Hale	13 May 1987
2882	Haley, Lillie D. R.		
		Horace F. Haley Jr.	13 Nov. 1945
1604	Hall, Jeanette R.		
		Harold S. Hall	6 Oct. 1931
1682	Hall, Minnie		
		Mark M. Hall	2 Apr. 1932
3483	Halma, Helen Mae		
		Hildebrand Halma	6 Feb. 1950
81210a	Hamilton, Carmen Ann		
		Richard Wilbur Hamilton	11 Feb. 1982
1711	Hamilton, Jarrell		
		Lorna Hamilton	23 Apr. 1932
84220a	Hamm, Rebecca Ann		
		Steven Phillip Hamm	12 Oct. 1984
3974	Hammonds, Sadie		
		Cleola Winfred Hammonds	15 July 1953
4590	Hammons, Florence Marie		
		Allen James Hammons	9 May 1958
2292	Hampson, Mabel		
		Jack Hampson	10 Mar. 1939
79175a	Hampton, Karen Elizabeth		
		Timothy Robison Hampton	13 Mar. 1980
83201a	Hanberry, Sallie Ann		
		Michael Wayne Hanberry	26 Apr. 1984
2482	Hand, Mary D.		
		David M. Hand	17 Nar. 1941
6050	Hansen, Alice		
		Richard Hansen	18 Oct. 1968
2819	Hansen, Doris		
		Harold C. Hansen	16 July 1945
5248	Hanson, Mary Catherine		
		Wm. Becker Hanson	8 Aug. 1966
81216a	Hanson, William Lee		
		Mary Williams Hanson	15 Jan. 1982
84271a	Hanus, Barbara Davis		
		Gary Lee Hanus	5 Dec. 1984
218	Hardee, Hanna H.		
		Jack Hardee	11 Nov. 1887

Case	Plaintiff	Defendant	Date
2906	Hardeman, Homer		
	Mae J. Hardeman		4 Mar. 1946
3946	Hardeman, Rosa Mae		
	James Hardeman		8 Sept. 1953
4266	Hardemon, Mary Ann		
	Obid Hardemon		7 Aug. 1956
5601	Hardemon, Mary Lee		
	John Hardemon Jr.		22 Dec. 1965
3814	Hardemon, Mary Lee		
	John Hardemon		8 Sept. 1952
5820	Harden, Frances Clare		
	Hollis C. Harden		30 Jan. 1967
84112a	Harden, Randol Philip		
	Kathleen Armstrong Harden		
			12 July 1984
5471	Harding, Vinnie Faye		
	Harold T. Harding		19 Mar. 1965
4661	Hardy, Katie		
	Ezra Hardy		18 Feb. 1959
3655	Hardy, Louise		
	Billy L. Hardy		26 Apr. 1951
79272a	Harley, Norma Lee Redish		
	Wm. Russell Harley		27 Feb. 1980
3073	Harper, Kenneth W.		
	Betty Jo Harper		2 Jan 1947
2577	Harrell, L. R.		
	Beatrice N. Harrell		10 Mar. 1942
5342	Harris, Curtis Franklin		
	Scarlet Lou Harris		29 May 1964
3653	Harris Johnnie F.		
	Annie Mae Harris		26 Apr. 1951
2777	Harris, Louise H.		
	Sidney M. Harris		5 Apr. 1945
1721	Harris, M. E.		
	Myrtle Thelma Harris		5 Oct. 1932
4689	Harris, Mary Louise W.		
	James M. Harris		2 Mar. 1959
2507	Harris, Nelene		
	Will Pope Harris		16 Sept. 1941
80254a	Harris, Peggy S.		
	Kenneth Royce Harris		2 Feb. 1981
2600	Harrison, Beuna M.		
	Elvis W. Harrison		28 Dec. 1941

54

Case	Plaintiff	Defendant	Date
2640	Harrison, Burma J.		
		Ruby J. Harrison	15 Mar. 1943
6010	Harrison, Florence M.		
		Morris D. Harrison	28 Feb. 1968
6054	Harrison, Joyce Lee		
		Hulett James Harrison	20 May 1968
82121a	Harrison, La Vonne M.		
		Forrest D. Harrison	8 Oct. 1982
5833	Harrison, Louada		
		William L. Harrison	8 Mar. 1967
7009	Harrison, Lynn Cooper		
		Robert Edward Harrison	19 June 1978
84259a	Harrison, Robt. Edward		
		Karen Kilgore Harrison	21 Nov. 1984
85147a	Harriss, Merri S.		
		William E. Harriss	11 Oct. 1985
2834	Harryman, Violet		
		James Wm. Harryman	16 July 1945
85304a	Hart, Linda Ball		
		Robert Earl Hart Jr.	13 Feb. 1986
87280a	Harthcock, Louie M.		
		Ozelia A. DeMasters Harthcock	
			20 Jan. 1988
5178	Hartley, Kathryn S.		
		Leslie E. Hartley	7 Mar. 1963
2182	Hartman, Anna M.		
		Roy G. Hartman	8 Mar 1938
2944	Hartmann, Lucille V.		
		Alois A. Hartmann	30 May 1946
2083	Hartmann, Myrtle		
		A. A. Hartmann	24 Oct. 1936
1648	Harvelle, Annette		
		W. B. Harvelle	7 Oct. 1931
8865a	Hasten, Shirley Bolton		
		Thomas Roy Hasten	19 Aug. 1988
5159	Hatcher, Martha Ann		
		Harold H. Hatcher	14 Dec. 1962
80265a	Hatton, Elnaria M.		
		Cafton Allen Hatton	20 Mar. 1981
88173a	Hawks, Cynthia D.		
		James E. Hawks	3 Feb. 1988
3447	Hawkins, Ruby		
		Tyrus Hawkins	13 Oct. 1949

Case	Plaintiff	Defendant	Date
1772	Hayden, Minnie C.		
		Nolan Hayden	20 Apr. 1933
8814a	Hazlett, Sylvia Annette		
		Daniel Marvin Hazelett	16 Mar. 1988
4439	Head, Jennie Dickey		
		Samuel Jackson Head	20 June 1957
4211	Heatley, Virginia		
		James l. Heatley	11 May 1955
4440	Heber, Reginald		
		Edythe R. Heber	27 Feb. 1957
1634	Heckler, Charles E.		
		Willie Mae Heckler	6 Oct. 1931
1601	Heckler, Charles E. Jr.		
		Tillie Heckler	4 Apr. 1931
2047	Heckler, Charles E. Jr.		
		Dora E. Heckler	6 Oct. 1936
5942	Hedrick, Emma E.		
		Lawton C. Hedrick	8 Sept. 1967
5713	Heffernan, Larry Gene		
		Cecilia Kay Heffernan	9 Aug. 1966
3074	Heimann, Ann		
		Louis Heimann Jr.	2 Jan. 1947
4382	Heimann, Dora		
		Jacob Heimann	29 Oct. 1956
2339	Heimann, Louis Jr.		
		Leila M. Heimann	3 Oct. 1939
4546	Heimann, Milton C.		
		Marian Heimann	8 Jan. 1958
8465a	Heinen, Lezlie Roger		
		Wayne Heinen	24 May 1984
4988	Helmke, Irma		
		Walter H. Helmke	15 June 1961
871a	Helms, Linda Lea		
		James Lee Helms	18 Mar. 1987
1870	Henard, Ollie Lee		
		Franklin Henard	11 Oct. 1934
82650a	Henderson, Barbara G.		
		Bobby E. Henderson	11 June 1982
2150	Henderson, C. E.		
		Gladys Henderson	24 Sept. 1937
1966	Henderson, F. E.		
		Willie Henderson	6 Apr. 1936
8792a	Henderson, Katherine Lynn		
		Jasper Ed. Henderson	8 July 1987

Case	Plaintiff	Defendant	Date
81238a	Henderson, Kathy Raye		
		Gary Lee Henderson	29 Jan. 1982
2704	Henderson, Lorine		
		L. K. Henderson Jr.	18 May 1944
6911	Henderson, Mercedes		
		Billy W. Henderson	19 May 1979
84200a	Henderson, Natha Jo		
		Aubrey Lynn Henderson	24 Jan. 1986
2609	Henderson, Ruby L.		
		L. K. Henderson	28 Dec. 1941
3843	Henderson, Sallie		
		J. E. Henderson	2 Sept. 1952
3614	Henderson, Welton		
		Jacquelyn L. Henderson	24 Apr. 1951
8491a	Hendrickson, Cynthia Lee		
		Ronald Dean Hendrickson	25 Oct. 1984
81257a	Henley, David Wayne		
		Justina S. Henley	21 Apr. 1982
8288a	Henley, Eva Marie		
		Jimmy Ray Henley Jr.	18 Mar. 1983
5390	Henley, Linda		
		Tommy Gene Henley	7 Oct. 1964
81155a	Henry, Dena Lee		
		Bill E. Henry	18 Nov. 1981
1732	Henry, Thelma		
		Byron S. Henry	11 Oct. 1932
5767	Henry, Virginia Cornar		
		Willy James Henry	9 Dec. 1966
79184a	Hensarling, Jo Emma		
		Robert Gene Hensarling	13 Dec. 1979
82232a	Hensley, Janie Jo		
		Patrick Roy Hensley	3 Feb, 1983
4284	Hensley, Mary Louise		
		Charles Hensley	16 Jan. 1956
7935a	Herbort, Pamela		
		Kenneth Herbirt	20 Apr. 1979
4015	Hereford, Bertha		
		Riese Hereford	7 Dec. 1953
3490	Hernandez, Corena F.		
		Jose F. Hernandez	26 June 1950
80152a	Hernandez, Deborah Parks		
		Jose Lopez Hernandez	29 Aug. 1980
2671	Hernandez, Higinia		
		Jesus Hernandez	7 Sept. 1943

Case	Plaintiff	Defendant	Date
2564	Hernandez, Josephine		
		Juan Hernandez	16 Dec. 1941
8266a	Hernandez, Teresa		
		Amelio Hernandez	12 Aug. 1982
1788	Herron, Eugene		
		Tinnie Herron	25 Oct. 1933
82294a	Herron, Judy Lynn Williams		
		Philip Don Herron	11 Jan 1983
4496	Hess, Mona Ruth		
		Ira Hess	26 Aug. 1957
8895a	Hesson, James Orbon		
		Nona Ballard Hesson	18 July 1988
3120	Heyland, Alma		
		Herman H. Heyland	9 June 1947
84134a	Heyen, Kathryn		
		Colby Joe Heyen	23 May 1985
3402	Heynen, Iva Jane R.		
		Harold W. Heynen	22 June 1949
2778	Hickman, Clarence M.		
		Meta Hickman	5 Apr. 1945
6149	Hicks, Virginia W.		
		William Parker Hicks	27 Nov. 1968
8287a	Highsmith, Charles Roger		
		Lizanna S. Veseeka Highsmith	
			2 Aug. 1982
5335	Highsmith, Vernadean		
		Lindsey F. Highsmith	28 May 1964
2896	Hightower, Wanda		
		John G. Hightower	5 June 1946
83247a	Hilburn, Shirley James		
		Norman L. Hilburn Sr.	9 Feb. 1984
81195a	Hill, A. D. Sr.		
		Brenda Jean Hill	20 Nov. 1981
6399	Hill, David Bernard		
		Carolee Pogoch Hill	15 May 1970
87294a	Hill, Don		
		Ginger L. Hill	15 Feb. 1989
3574	Hill, Edward B.		
		Edna Hill	11 Sept. 1950
83155a	Hill, Faye Elizabeth		
		William Virgil Hill	15 Sept. 1983
6157	Hill, Frances F.		
		William Kenneth Hill	27 Dec. 1968

Case	Plaintiff	Defendant	Date
3321	Hillmer, Merle		
		G. L. Hillmer	22 Nov. 1948
86169a	Hilmers, Harlen H.		
		Pauletta Hilmers	3 Dec. 1986
8545a	Hind, Dorothy Jean		
		Gary James Hind	20 Sept. 1985
3154	Hobbs, Mary		
		W. S. Hobbs	5 Aug. 1947
3725	Hobson, Dolly Ealer		
		Earl Hobson	10 Oct. 1951
85298a	Hodge, Isabell		
		Steven Glenn Hodge	15 Apr. 1986
1890	Hodges, Don N.		
		Willie Hodges	22 Oct. 1934
2483	Hodges, Elizabeth		
		Harmon Hodges	17 Sept. 1940
5618	Hodges, Maybelle G.		
		James R. Hodges	7 July 1988
2949	Hodges, Vivian		
		Kirby Hodges	23 Apr. 1946
2710	Hoffman, Ethel		
		Arthur Hoffman	18 May 1944
85193a	Hoffman, Wanda Faye Jones		
		Robt. Luse Hoffman	27 Sept. 1985
3279	Hoggett, Roberta J.		
		Jack C. Hoggett	7 Sept. 1948
2878	Hohenberger, Bruno		
		Maud Hohenberger	30 May 1946
3577	Holcomb, Faye		
		William Jeff Holcomb	28 Nov. 1950
1699	Holden, Elizabeth		
		Emmett Holden	28 Mar. 1933
2141	Holden, Elizabeth		
		Emmett Holden	28 Sept. 1937
4141	Hollan, Josephine Woods		
		Harley A. Hollan	6 Dec. 1954
3125	Holland, Annie Mae		
		Otto Buford Holland	13 May 1947
5911	Holley, Hannah Corene Dean		
		Thomas Eldon Holley	24 July 1967
4611	Holliman, Doris Onita		
		Eiley Ray Holliman	2 June 1958
2680	Holliman, Vera Lee		
		Walter Holliman	6 Sept. 1943

Case	Plaintiff	Defendant	Date
6400	Hollimon, Mary E.		
		Ray E. Hollimon	9 Apr. 1971
5365	Hollmes, Beverly		
		Robert Holmes	13 July 1964
86183a	Holness, Carolyn		
		J. M. Holness	18 Feb. 1987
2247	Holloman, Agnes		
		Roger Holloman	3 Oct. 1938
82129a	Holloway, Cindy Sue		
		Raymond Powell Holloway	24 Sept. 1982
7863a	Holloway, William Rudolph Jr.		
		Aleta Mae Holloway	21 Mar. 1979
2824	Holman, Marjorie		
		Hubert Holman	10 Dec. 1945
6949	Holmes, Beverly Ann		
		Elisha Eugene Holmes	9 Nov. 1977
3702	Holt, Catherine Lucille		
		Donald Ray Holt	5 Sept. 1951
6197	Hamilton, Rosalyn Diane		
		Clyde E. Hamilton	23 July 1969
85159a	Honeycutt, Lisa Kay		
		Larry Joe Hunnycutt	27 Sept. 1985
4771	Hooker, Ethel Elizabeth		
		James Wesley Hooker	2 Dec. 1959
4941	Hooker, James Wesley		
		Myril Hill	19 Dec. 1960
6047	Hooten, Elvera		
		James W. Hooten	17 Sept. 1968
4078	Horn, Winnie		
		Homer Clinton Horn	28 July 1954
131	Hornbeck, Sarah E.		
		Duval Hornbeck	9 Nov. 1882
80190a	Horton, Robert Edward		
		Donna Renee Horton	2 Feb. 1981
4770	Houck, Donald Julian		
		Virginia Lee Houck	29 Aug. 1959
89121a	Howard, Barbara Joan		
		Vernon lee Howard	2 Sept. 1981
83227a	Howard, Charles O. Jr.		
		Catherine J. Howard	24 Feb. 1984
4509	Howard, Homer Eugene		
		Mertie Pearl Howard	19 May 1958
1685	Howard, Ira Mabel		
		Chas. Oscar Howard	28 Mar. 1932

Case	Plaintiff Defendant	Date
79276a	Howard, Laura Jane Stephen L. Howard	9 July 1980
6355	Howard, Mattie Nelson Robert George Howard	20 Oct. 1969
87217a	Howard, Nancy Leah Linn Mark Howard	18 Nov. 1987
5429	Howard, Susan Elizabeth Joe Mack Howard	19 May 1965
5033	Howarth, Dale William Dean Martin Howarth	19 Sept. 1961
81190a	Howarth, Edith Louise Dale W. Howarth	20 Nov. 1981
81181a	Howell, Barbara Ann Bobby Bane Howell	20 Nov. 1981
86244a	Howell, Delbert Lee Brenda Gwen Howell	18 Mar. 1987
5579	Howell, Dixie Pearle James Franklin Howell	16 May 1966
2491	Howell, Jewel Clarence Howell	25 Mar. 1941
4833	Howell, Joyce Elaine Jimmy Walker Howell	16 Feb. 1960
85135a	Howell, Mary Beaver Bobby Blaine Howell	6 Aug. 1985
4389	Howell, Nettie Jean Robert Lee Howell	24 Sept. 1957
1683	Howett, Lillie William Howett	4 Oct. 1932
87130a	Huang, Kuo Ying Fong Ching Ming Huang	17 Sept. 1987
81134a	Huber, Mary Magdalen Edward Harry Huber Jr.	3 Spet. 1981
8438a	Hudson, Pattie Mark Davis Hudson	6 Apr. 1984
8393a	Hueske, Edward E. May Ann Hueske	18 Aug. 1983
84313a	Hueske, Eva Edward E. Hueske	24 Jan 1985
4690	Hughes, Barbara Eltha Chas. Stewart Hughes	8 Dec. 1958
3328	Hughes, Belle Alva Hughes	7 Feb. 1949
3550	Hughes, Hazel Ewell F. Hughes	25 July 1950

Case	Plaintiff	Defendant	Date
2992	Hughes, Opal		
		F. H. Hughes	15 Feb. 1947
2508	Humphrey, Adell		
		Jack E. Humphrey	25 Aug. 1941
5561	Hunphries, Virgil Leo		
		Mary Humphries	5 Oct. 1965
2912	Hunt, Charles E.		
		Amerilla Hunt	25 Feb. 1946
4011	Hunt, Frankie		
		Earl Max Hunt	17 Dec. 1953
5717	Hurley, Jennie Buck		
		Roy J. Hurley	21 Sept. 1966
78107a	Hurst, James Albert		
		Brenda Fay Hurst	4 Jan. 1979
5105	Hurst, Jones A.		
		Neita Sue Hurst	4 June 1962
5000a	Hurst, Juanita		
		Lloyd B. Hurst	8 Nov. 1961
6973	Hurst, Sharon Garmes		
		Jerrel Aubrey Hurst Jr.	
			18 Dec. 1977
6000	Hutchison, Larayne C.		
		Jerry W. Hutchison	27 May 1970
2960	Hutson, Daniel A.		
		Esta Mae Hutson	30 June 1946
5052	Hux, Opal Jacquline		
		Joe E. Hux	5 Jan. 1962
6215	Hyatt, Clara Mae		
		Carl Ray Hyatt	20 May 1969
84122a	Hyatt, Douglas Ray		
		Cheryl Lee Hyatt	16 July 1984
4985	Hyde, Bennie Marshall		
		Alma Yvonne Moore Kiderell Hyde	
			25 July 1961
4652	Hyde, Clarence		
		Helen Hyde	10 Sept. 1958
85316a	Hyde, Margurita B.		
		Thomas C. Hyder	18 Mar. 1986
2138	Hyde, Mary		
		John B. Hyde	4 Oct. 1937
6112	Hyde, Ray A.		
		Ben J. Hyde	4 Nov. 1968
80114a	Hyde, Thomas C.		
		Sandra L. Hyde	1 Aug. 1980

Case	Plaintiff	Defendant	Date
2534	Hyde, Viola P.		
	Benjamin J. Hyde		19 Sept. 1941
5324	Hysaw, Vera Lee		
	Willie Clarence Hysaw		29 May 1964

I

Case	Plaintiff	Defendant	Date
4903	Idlebird, Rele		
	Della Mae Idlebird		16 Sept. 1960
8055a	Ingenhuett, Rita E.		
	Dennis E. Ingenhuett		20 May 1981
2376	Ingle, Alfred G.		
	Frances M. Ingle		28 Mar. 1980
4246	Ingram, Lena Maye		
	Marron Doyle Ingram		11 Jan. 1956
2638	Ingram, Mary M.		
	A. A. (Star) Ingram		15 Mar. 1943
2230	Innes, William H.		
	Laura Innes		8 Oct. 1938
6224	Irving, Elvin R.		
	Elveta R. Irving		24 July 1969
79153a	Isenberg, Elizabeth Patrica Culton		
	Joe Alan Isenberg		3 Jan. 1980

J

Case	Plaintiff	Defendant	Date
5388	Jackson, Edna Benson		
	Willie Lee Jackson		9 Apr. 1965
5377	Jackson, Essie		
	Nathan Jackson		1 Sept. 1964
2900	Jackson, George		
	Janie Jackson		25 Feb. 1946
2239	Jackson, Gladys		
	Lane Jackson		26 Sept. 1938
8337a	Jackson, Hattie M.		
	Ricky D. Jackson		25 May 1983
3059	Jackson, Jessie		
	Louise Jackson		2 Jan. 1947
2434	Jackson. John		
	Ella Jackson		31 Oct. 1940

Case	Plaintiff	Defendant	Date
1	Jackson, Oliver		
		Lena Jackson	25 Oct. 1870
3703	James, Billie		
		Arlie R. James	10 Sept. 1951
3048	James, Billie Lou		
		Gerald James	25 Oct. 1946
3611	James, Edith		
		Billy C. James	30 Jan 1951
3320	James, Gerald C.		
		Doris James	22 Nov. 1948
4035	James, Hillery		
		Alberta James	1 Feb 1954
8494a	James Raylene Maria		
		Michael Vincent James	21 June 1984
2575	James, S. N.		
		Edna James	10 Mar. 1942
87170a	Janson, Elizabeth		
		Charles Janson	17 Feb. 1988
3132	Jarrett, Jessie		
		Wayne Jarrett	9 June 1947
83160a	Jeffers, Deanna Lynn		
		Donald Lee Jeffers	9 Aug. 1983
6142	Jeffers, Jewel Ellen		
		John Jeffers	24 Jan. 1969
85189a	Jeffers, Walter Henry		
		Laverne Emma Jeffers	27 Sept. 1985
83217a	Jefferson, Pamela Kay		
		Jack W. Jefferson	3 Feb. 1984
4074	Jenkins, Ann		
		Rufus Jenkins	14 Sept. 1954
3617	Jenkins, Lorene		
		Arvid Lee Jenkins	18 June 1951
8281a	Jenschke, Cheryl Dawn		
		Lawrence James Jenschke	2 Aug. 1982
8282a	Jimenez, Gilbert John		
		Juanita Rios Jimenez	23 July 1982
5785	Jobes, Agnes Rosie		
		William Wayne Jobes	2 Dec. 1966
4212	Jobes, William W.		
		Lena Ruth Jobes	5 Sept. 1955
4229	Johnson, Adell		
		J. F. Johnson	12 Aug. 1955
6059	Johnson, Beverly Morris		
		Harold Zay Johnson	4 Aug. 1969

Case	Plaintiff	Defendant	Date
8033a	Johnson, Eugenia		
		Tommy J. Johnson	16 May 1980
3126	Johnson, Faye		
		R. L. Johnson	10 June 1947
88267a	Johnson Karl Anthony		
		Patricia Norma Johnson	30 Oct. 1991
87291a	Johnson, Kristi Lynn		
		John Mark Johnson	18 Jan. 1990
2885	Johnson, Lucille		
		John J. Johnson	10 Dec. 1945
84267a	Johnson, Paul Douglas		
		Cathy Sue Johnson	22 Oct. 1985
3766	Johnson, Rose Mills		
		Leonard Johnson	27 Mar. 1952
6252	Johnson, Sylvia J.		
		Eldon W. Johnson	22 July 1969
1593	Jonas, Ada Birt		
		William Jonas	30 Mar. 1931
1710	Jonas, Opal May		
		William J. Jonas	29 Mar. 1932
1854	Jonas, Opal May		
		W. J. (Bill) Jonas	12 Apr. 1934
3406	Jones, Alvin		
		Louise Jones	18 July 1949
82144a	Jones, Cynthia Dickey		
		Donald Eugene Jones	21 Oct. 1983
8641a	Jones, Donna Leah		
		Billy Mack Jones	15 Apr. 1986
1609	Jones, Edna		
		Rodney Jones	25 Apr. 1931
3356	Jones, Ethel		
		James H. Jones	23 May 1949
2101	Jones, Fanny Jane		
		Clint Jones	30 Mar. 1937
786a	Jones, Frances Marie		
		Harold O'Dean Jones	28 Aug. 1978
2817	Jones, Frank M.		
		Mary Lee Jones	8 June 1945
3212	Jones, Frankie		
		Ernest Jones	13 Apr. 1953
5850	Jones, James M.		
		Susie May Jones	3 Apr. 1967
79136a	Jones, Janet Billings		
		Terry Jay Jones	4 Oct. 1979

Case	Plaintiff	Defendant	Date
3878	Jones, Jewel		
		Margaret Jones	9 Feb. 1953
4579	Jones, Juanita		
		James D. Jones Jr.	25 Mar. 1958
80256a	Jones, Judith Sezanne		
		Michael Hasting Jones	27 Jan. 1981
8496a	Jones, Kay Ann		
		Joe Donovan Jones	30 Aug. 1984
6903	Jones, Lee Anne		
		James Carlton Jones	20 July 1979
3743	Jones, Louise		
		Alvin Jones	7 Dec. 1951
3602	Jones, Lucretia		
		Walter R. Jones	19 Dec. 1950
4607	Jones, Marvel W.		
		Richard E. Jones Jr.	30 May 1958
2563	Jones, Mary J.		
		A. T. Jones	11 Mar. 1942
5247	Jones, Nadine Lorine		
		Lindsey Rudolph Jones	9 Sept. 1963
5200	Jordan, Dora Le Ray		
		Birdie Allen Jordan	19 June 1964
4048	Jordan, Margaret Ruth		
		Charles Ray Jordan	2 Apr. 1954
3386	Joshua, Edward		
		Florine Joshua	24 May 1949
4808	Joy, Ethel Lee		
		William Ira Joy	21 Dec. 1959
3464	Joy, Karl E.		
		Vivian Joy	13 Dec. 1949
3088	Joy, W. I.		
		Roberta Joy	26 Mar. 1947
2965	Juarez, Benita		
		Santos Juarez	5 June 1946
4582	Juarez, Raymond Z.		
		Marian Juarez	1 Apr. 1958
80191a	Jung, Bertha Cruz		
		Gilbert Del Valle Jung	21 Nov. 1980
83165a	Jung, Cathy Loreann		
		Keith Alan Jung	14 Oct. 1983
3091	Jushua, Edward		
		Della Mae Jushua	13 June 1947

Case	Plaintiff	Defendant	Date

K

Case	Plaintiff / Defendant	Date
82270a	Kadkhodazadeh, Ana Villaneuva Hossein Kadkhodazadah	18 Feb. 1983
4534	Kahey, Hiram Aileen Kahey	13 Jan. 1958
8785a	Kain, Carole Ann Karson Adrain Kain	18 June 1985
5261	Kaiser, Carol Frank Kaiser	14 Oct. 1963
7860a	Kaiser, Frederick E. Barbara Ann Kaiser	17 Nov. 1978
81225a	Kaiser, Kathleen Steven Wayne Kaiser	31 Dec. 1981
6471	Kane, Joyce G. W. Kane	3 Feb. 1972
2953	Kane, Thelma L. G. W. Kane	5 June 1946
8466a	Kaufhold, Dawn Louise Harold Henry Kaufhold Jr.	27 Aug. 1984
4586	Keese, Esther Willie Gerald Keese	9 May 1958
2311	Keiffer, Max Willie G. Keiffer	24 Mar. 1939
6041	Kelch, Irene Schulz Hubert Kelch	10 June 1968
5003a	Kelch, Ruth Hubert Kelch	8 Aug. 1962
8557a	Keller, Darla Bowers Stephen A. Keller	3 Dec. 1986
82111a	Keller, Kay Edwin N. Keller Jr.	5 Nov. 1982
78134a	Keller, Mary Ruth Maulding Wm. Powell Keller	18 May 1979
8460a	Keller, Patricia Elaine Edwin Niel Keller Jr.	24 May 1984
2431	Kelley, Birdie Hy Kelley	18 Sept. 1940
84360a	Kelly, Gail Ann Bobby Ray Kelly	6 Mar. 1985
3021	Kelly, Hazel Dale Kelly	3 Sept. 1946

Case	Plaintiff	Defendant	Date
3310	Kelsey, Hazel O.		
		Melvin K. Kelsey	9 Feb. 1949
1961	Kemp, Mineola		
		Roy Kemp	18 Oct. 1935
6932	Kemper, Doris Jean		
		Hugh Clinton Kemper	16 Nov. 1977
2142	Kendall, Anna Mae		
		Walter W. Kendall	22 Sept. 1937
5257	Kendall, Claude Anderson		
		Betty Kendall	16 Oct. 1963
5981	Kendall, Ruby P.		
		Wayne E. Kendall	11 July 1968
4156	Kendall, W. W.		
		Nora Kendall	9 Feb. 1955
4418	Kennedy, Evangeline		
		Charles R. Culver Kennedy	
			14 June 1959
3945	Kennedy, Marian Wood		
		John Robert Kennedy	15 July 1953
5051	Kenner, Donald B.		
		Catherine L. Kenner	8 Jan. 1962
5328	Kensing, Monroe E.		
		Frankie E. Kensing	4 Jan. 1965
4721	Keonnecke, Estella		
		Arthur Keonnecke	29 May 1959
4588	Kiliszewski, Alma Ella		
		Walter Kiliszewski	7 Oct. 1959
5886	Kiliszewski, Clara Nimmo		
		Walter A. Kiliszewski	13 Oct. 1967
8589a	Kimble, Barbara Kay		
		James Leo Kimble	25 June 1985
80231a	Kincade, Jo Brenda		
		Wm. Albert Kincade	12 Oct. 1984
4184	Kincaid, Frank T.		
		Joan Bell Kincaid	11 May 1955
4925	Kincheloe, Peggy H.		
		Lee Roy kincheloe	4 Jan. 1961
6419	King, Ethel C.		
		Carroll King	9 June 1970
82179a	King, Patrick Cowden		
		Shawn Lynn King	3 Dec. 1982
82112a	King, Ruth Carol		
		Richard David King	30 Aug. 1982

Case	Plaintiff	Defendant	Date
3459	King, Samuel		
		Orlace Orene King	12 Dec. 1949
80268a	King, Sherry M.		
		Frank Snyder King Jr.	3 Feb. 1981
1780.5	Kingsbury, Dorothy E.		
		J. J. Kingsbury	26 Oct. 1933
3975	Kinser, Evelyn		
		George A. Kinser Jr.	17 Sept. 1953
3536	Kinsey, Lucille		
		O. W. Kinsey	26 June 1950
4201	Kinsey, Lucy		
		O. W. Kinsey	22 Sept. 1955
3638	Kinsey, Lucy Orlanda		
		Otho William Kinsey	25 Apr. 1951
5150	Kirchhoff, Aleene		
		Leroy Kirchhoff	11 Jan. 1963
5745	Kirchhoff, Leroy		
		Mary Jane Kirchhoff	21 Sept. 1966
8972	Kirkland, Lucretia Jean		
		Charles Anderson Kirkland	
			19 Jan. 1978
78157a	Kitchens, Debra Cannon		
		Michael Raymond Kitchens	
			16 Mar. 1979
3639	Kitto, Anita		
		Frank Kitto	23 Apr. 1951
80140a	Kitzner, Claudia M.		
		Alvin E. Kitzner	30 Dec. 1980
80177a	Kizer, Roy David Jr.		
		Gloria Janelle Kizer	30 Mar. 1981
4989	Klech, Adolph		
		Jean Eliz. Klech	25 July 1961
5670	Klein, Frances Joe		
		Kenneth Karl Klein	28 Apr. 1966
5891	Klein, Kenneth Karl		
		Frances Jo Klein	9 Aug. 1967
1926	Klein, Mary		
		Walter Klein	26 Apr. 1935
84235a	Klein, W. C. Jr.		
		Iona Mae Burnet Klein	25 June 1985
6221	Kline, Isla Mae		
		Morriss Phillip Kline	16 May 1969
8439a	Klingemann, Bernadette A.		
		Robert C. Klingemann	6 Apr. 1984

Case	Plaintiff	Defendant	Date
6972	Klingemann, Peggy Gene		
		Robert Charles Klingemann	
			3 Jan. 1978
2259	Knapp, Georgia P.		
		Dwight R. Knapp	3 Apr. 1946
7844a	Kneese, Ada Louise		
		Travis Donald Kneese	19 Oct. 1978
4923	Kneese, Amanda Klaehn		
		Wilmer W. Kneese	5 Oct. 1960
6162	Kneese, Judith N.		
		Royce G. Kneese	13 Feb. 1969
8234a	Kneese, Linda Gayleen		
		Gary Grant Kneese	11 June `1982
84182a	Kneip, Karen Fay		
		Delvin Wayne Kneip	16 Aug. 1984
5987	Knight, Lori Ann		
		Alton Knight	8 Jan. 1968
5279	Knox, Anne Belle		
		Leroy Coleman Knox	17 Dec. 1963
8574a	Knox, Carol J.		
		Charles Duane Knox	13 Aug. 1985
4006	Knox, Dorothy		
		Charles Knox	17 Dec. 1953
2260	Knox, Edna		
		George Knox	4 Oct. 1938
4778	Knox, Johnny		
		Bertha Knox	26 Feb. 1959
2963.5	Knox, Lucille		
		J. M. Knox	26 Apr. 1946
2118	Knox, Maudie		
		George Knox	30 Jan. 1937
2542	Knox, R. L.		
		G. C. Knox	25 Mar. 1942
4012	Koch, Ella Crenwelge		
		C. F. Koch	7 Dec. 1953
2484	Koehler, Norma Gene		
		Louis Koehler	2 Mar. 1941
2384	Koennecke, Mary L.		
		C. Koennecke	5 Mar. 1940
4897	Kokes, Lloyd		
		Hattie Kokes	23 Nov. 1960
8849a	Kolacek, Ann Margaret Smith		
		Eddie Dale Kolacek	6 Sept. 1989

Case	Plaintiff	Defendant	Date
8785a	Kosma, Patricia Elaine		
		David Alan Kosma	29 July 1987
80123a	Kott, Melvin Hilmer Jr.		
		Helen Katherine Kott	2 Oct. 1980
8422a	Kramer, Billy Joe		
		Brenda Lucille Louis Kramer	
			26 Apr. 1984
3400	Kremer, William H.		
		Helen Kremer	18 July 1949
85165a	Krey, William T.		
		Nancy Lee Krey	19 Dec. 1985
834a	Krischke, Brenda Lou		
		Richard Kendall Krischke	
			9 May 1983
1741	Kroenert, Hilda		
		George Kroenert Jr.	28 Apr. 1933
7976a	Kuhlmann, Jimmy		
		Vivian Alice Kuhlmann	16 May 1984
2312	Kuleff, Ann		
		Pete Kuleff	24 Mar. 1939
80224a	Kunz, Pamela Marie		
		Charles H. Kunz	16 Jan 1981
79277a	Kurtz, Teresa Joann		
		Louis Thos. Kurtz	31 Mar. 1980
5074	Kutschke, Helen Wehra		
		Charles Kutschke	26 Jan. 1962
4044	Kutzer, Helen		
		Charles Kutzer	2 Apr. 1954
3255	Kutzer, J. A.		
		Helen Mae Kutzer	14 June 1948
4196	Kutzer, Ruby		
		Jesse A. Kutzer	9 Apr. 1955

L

Case	Plaintiff	Defendant	Date
81182a	La Bounty, Donald A.		
		Reube M. La Bounty	29 Oct. 1981
5423	Lacey, Jack		
		Annie Mae Lacey	8 Jan. 1965
3349	Lackaby, Lee		
		Opal Lackaby	7 Feb. 1949
8263a	Lackey, Alyce Maye		
		Vinton Lee Lackey	11 June 1982

Case	Plaintiff	Defendant	Date
5591	Lackey, Bessie		
		Leslie G. Lackey	20 Nov. 1965
802a	Lackey, Edward Keith		
		Le Ann Kenam Lackey	18 Apr. 1980
8494a	Lackey, Edward Keith		
		Crida Charlene Lackey	27 Sept. 1985
81221a	Lackey, Elsie Sue		
		Earl Calvin Lackey	10 June 1983
5720	Lackey, Janice Marie		
		Gordon B. Lackey	8 Aug. 1966
2840	Lackey, Leona		
		Elmer Lackey	5 Sept. 1945
3741	Lackey, Leona		
		Pete Lackey	18 Dec. 1951
8224a	Lackey, Leota Anna		
		John Onar Lackey	8 Oct. 1982
4020	Lackey, Ruby		
		J. C. Lackey	7 Dec. 1953
5337	Lackey, Sue Smith		
		B. F. Lackey III	21 May 1964
84326a	Lackey, Tommy Howard		
		Jo Ann Lackey	9 Apr. 1985
85134a	Ladd, Lynn		
		Vernon H. Ladd Jr.	28 Aug. 1985
79183a	Lafferty, Leona Marie		
		Kenny Earl Lafferty	27 Feb. 1980
3066	Laing, Dorothy Mae		
		Charles L. Laing	3 Feb. 1947
3445	Lainhart, Virginia L.		
		John C. Lainhart	12 Oct. 1949
78123a	Lamb, Violet L.		
		Bennett G. Lamb	14 May 1980
4144	Lambert, Gladys Merle		
		Nolan Lester Lambert	24 Dec. 1954
80246a	Lambert, Stewart B.		
		Dorothy Diane Lambert	20 May 1983
6124	Land, Geraldine		
		Charles R. Land	28 July 1970
829a	Land, Marie Parks Mc Daniel		
		Chas. Russell Land	24 May 1982
88271a	Landin, Ramiro Garza		
		Berta Ybarra Landin	1 Nov. 1989
6941	Lane, John B. Sr.		
		Wanda Mae Lane	19 Jan. 1978

Case	Plaintiff	Defendant	Date
----	Lane, Margaret B. M. Lane		11 Nov. 1861
51	Lane, Margaret B. W. Lane		11 Nov. 1861
8729a	Lane, Susan Mary Mc Nair Allen Lane		22 Apr. 1989
5347	Lang, Edwin H. Leola H. Lang		10 June 1964
3082	Lang, Mary Doke W. G. Lange		26 Mar. 1947
4468	Langdon, Nell E. Jesse Langdon Jr.		25 Mar. 1958
3078	Lange, Mary E. Travis D. Lange		3 Feb. 1947
6381	Lange, Tommie L. Ed. J. Lange		11 Mar. 1970
3481	Lange, W. G. Mathilda Lange		1 Dec. 1950
3953	Langford, Joe W. Mary Lou Robbins Langford		7 Sept. 1954
79243a	Lanier, Dolly Ann Castle Jeffery Amort Lanier		14 Feb. 1980
3118	Lankford, Bertha Stanley Lankford		9 June 1947
3013	Lantz, Mattie E. S. Lantz		25 Oct. 1946
8327a	La Porte, Michelle D. Danny M. La Porte		5 May 1983
85142a	Lara, Anne Marie Jesse Lara		18 Sept. 1985
3612	Lara, Cecilio E. Lilly Lara		24 Apr. 1951
3284	Lara, Juaquin Concha Lara		25 Oct. 1948
6095	Lara, Natalia Raymond Lara		8 Aug. 1968
8610a	Lara, Vincent N. Laura N. Lara		24 Mar. 1986
5982	Latour, Wilson Beatrice Latour		2 June 1969
3004	Lavaul, Joyce Eddie F. Lavaul		3 Feb. 1947

Case	Plaintiff	Defendant	Date
4431	Lawdermilk, Chanos R.		
		Manda Vernice Lawdermilk	
			16 Jan. 1957
1630	Lawson, Lucia		
		Clarence Lawson	22 Dec. 1931
6342	Leach, Patsy L.		
		Stephen B. Leach	20 Feb. 1970
5688	Leathermann, Opal		
		Herman O. Leathermann	7 July 1966
3041	Leatherwood, Robert D.		
		Fannie Leatherwood	9 June 1947
3338	Leatherwood, Robert D.		
		Barbara J. Leatherwood	20 Dec. 1948
1624	Leavell, A. M.		
		Pearl Mae Leavell	18 Apr. 1931
2229	Leavell, A. M.		
		Ann J. Leavell	3 Oct. 1938
84304a	Lee, Delores F.		
		Hopkins B. Lee	11 July 1985
7995a	Lee, Etta Lynn Mc Grew		
		Glenn Monroe Lee	9 July 1979
2226	Lee, Fannie Jane		
		Leo Lee	20 Sept. 1938
2590	Lee, Mildred		
		Thomas J. Lee	17 Apr. 1942
3095	Lee, Victor B.		
		Lorenza Lee	14 Apr. 1947
3607	Lee, Virginia B.		
		Jack W. Lee	18 May 1951
1619	Leeder, Edwin		
		Eleanor Leeder	23 Apr. 1931
2354	Legg, Ilyne		
		Gene Legg	2 Oct. 1939
79185a	Lehman, David		
		Cynthia Bills Lehman	12 Nov. 1979
87108a	L'Huilleur, John Paul		
		Gladys Stutts L'Huilleur	13 Aug. 1987
2983	Leinweber, Tidy M.		
		Max G. Leinweber	30 May 1946
6864	Leinweber, Ollie Agnes		
		Max Garland Leinweber	15 Dec. 1977
86186a	Leissner, Gary Alan		
		Nita Bob Mc Millam Leissner	
			28 Dec. 1988

Case	Plaintiff	Defendant	Date
78129a	Le Meilleur, Charles David		
		Mary Ann Le Meilleur	30 Mar. 1979
83222a	Le Meilleur, Raymond Scott		
		Doris Mae Le Meilleur	23 Mar. 1989
3165	Lemley, Mary L.		
		Miles Charles Lemley	4 Sept. 1947
2397	Lenord, Allie Lee		
		Thalis O. Lenord	27 Mar. 1940
4595	Leonard, Clarence		
		Ophelia Leonard	1 May 1958
4007	Leonard, Geneva		
		Archie L. Leonard	7 Dec. 1953
83163a	Leonard, Vickie Ann		
		James Elton Leonard	14 Oct. 1983
2662	Levingston, Irene		
		Lou J. Levingston	8 Sept. 1943
6396	Lewis, Larry R.		
		Maria Olga Lewis	1 Apr. 1970
4285	Leyendecker, Ruth D.		
		Michael M Leyendecker Jr.	
			3 Jan. 1956
6302	Lich, Agnes C.		
		Roy D. Lich	23 Oct. 1969
1625	Liles, Nolen		
		Norma Liles	6 Oct. 1931
8352a	Lilly, Dan A.		
		Kathleen Margaret Lilly	24 Feb. 1984
7027	Lindsey, Katherine Ann		
		Thomas Gregory Lindsey	31 Aug. 1978
1605	Link, Millie		
		J. W. Link	31 Mar. 1931
2871	Linn, Barbara J.		
		Joe B. Linn	13 Nov. 1945
79273a	Linney, Rebecca Jean		
		Lowell F. Linney	15 Feb. 1980
82217a	Lira, Pilar Martinez		
		Felix Lira	17 Dec. 1982
7929a	Little, Mary Kathryn		
		Mitchell James Little	6 July 1979
5524	Littlefield, Viola		
		P. E. Littlefield	28 June 1965
4947	Lockaby, Jennie Belle		
		Lee W. Lochaby	23 May 1961

Case	Plaintiff	Defendant	Date
1628	Loesberg, George		
		Grace Loesberg	6 Oct. 1931
5037	Loesburg, Elmer Lee		
		Beverly Jean Loesburg	14 Mar. 1964
5297	Logan, Mary		
		Vernon W. Logan	13 Jan. 1964
3084	Long, Bruce		
		Fay Long	3 Feb. 1947
3127	Long, Charlotte Anna		
		Lawrence M. Long	14 June 1948
8549a	Long, Cynthia Marie		
		Mark Andrew Long	25 June 1985
1937	Lopez, Conception		
		Jesus Lopez	8 Oct. 1935
2966	Lopez, Eva		
		Raul Lopez	5 June 1946
78117a	Lopez, Helen Annis		
		Julio Mirelos Lopez	28 Feb. 1979
4947	Lopez, Hope		
		Albert Lopez	19 Apr. 1960
87101a	Lopez, Ramon		
		Maribel S. Lopez	29 Aug. 1987
84137a	Losey, Winona Sue Smith		
		Emerson Max Losey	19 Sept. 1984
5278	Lott, Betty Hazelle		
		Lewis J. Lott	19 Mar. 1965
4060	Lott, Dorotha		
		Lewis J. Lott	14 May 1954
8483a	Lott, Iona Grace		
		Marvin Tracy Lott	8 June 1984
4624	Lott, Margaret G.		
		Gilbert Lott	14 Oct. 1968
5913	Lott, Molly Sue		
		Michael L. Lott	2 Aug. 1967
5239	Lott, Oleane		
		Albert E. Lott	20 Aug. 1963
4990	Lott, Walter		
		Lois Juanita Lott	8 June 1961
4028	Lott, William R.		
		Rosie Lee Lott	2 Feb. 1954
2991	Love, Alexander J.		
		Pauline Love	20 June 1946
7859a	Love, Frances Naomi		
		Robert Earl Love	1 Nov. 1978

Case	Plaintiff / Defendant	Date
2290	Love, Geneva Jeff Love	21 Mar. 1939
8781a	Love, Irene Robin Robt. Dewayne Love	8 July 1987
2620	Love, Mary Lee Duncan D. Love	8 Mar. 1943
88273a	Love, Robert E. Jr. Vickey Bessent Love	15 Feb. 1989
7921a	Love, Robert Earl Sarah Nell Love	2 May 1979
5386	Loving, Mariann N. B. D. Loving	15 Jan. 1965
3556	Low, Marjorie Y. T. B. Low Jr.	25 Aug. 1950
6146	Low, Pricilla Baker T. B. Low Jr.	19 Nov. 1968
4220	Lowrance, J. E. Margaret Lowrance	27 Mar. 1956
2762	Lowrance, Mae Silas E. Lowrance	19 Dec. 1944
4079	Lowrance, Viola Lee James E. Lowrance	28 May 1954
3722	Lozano, Bicenta Rafael Lozano	18 Dec. 1951
2731	Lozano, Juan Modesta Lozano	5 Sept. 1944
2211	Lozano, Raymond Concha Lozano	21 Sept. 1938
1707	Lucas, Norvella J. D. Lucas	22 Dec. 1931
4176	Lueders, Bertha Lee Melvin Leroy Luedes	11 May 1955
3141	Lumpkin, Bernice John Lumpkin	10 June 1947
3651	Lumpkin, Madeline John M. Lumpkin	12 Sept. 1951
83229a	Lunsford, Judy Ann James Douglas Lunsford	12 Oct. 1984
6106	Luther, Louise James Luther	21 Aug. 1968
4029	Luxton, Billie Carol Everett Edward Luxton	2 Feb. 1954
6245	Lyle, Rudene E. Ed W. Lyle	13 Aug. 1969

Case	Plaintiff	Defendant	Date
8889a	Lynch, Eva Ann		
		David Eugene Lynch	14 July 1988
889a	Lynn, Gerald David		
		Tyeoka Ann Lynn	6 Apr. 1988

M

Case	Plaintiff	Defendant	Date
3491	Mac Donald, Paul		
		Ora T. Mac Donald	19 Apr. 1950
2151	Machen, Inez		
		Thomas Machen	8 Mar. 1938
4822	Machen, Juanita		
		Wm. Benj. Machen	11 Feb. 1960
2475	Mack, Frank		
		Nannie Mae Mack	11 Mar. 1941
88257a	Mack, Helen Louise Spitz		
		Archie Charley Mack	25 Jan 1989
6259	Maddox, Darrel Preston		
		Clarabell Maddox	2 Oct. 1969
2382	Madrano, Maria		
		Juan B. Madrano	6 Mar. 1940
7920a	Magee, David W.		
		Joy Nell Magee	23 Jan. 1980
85271a	Magee, Norah		
		Phil R. Magee III	11 July 1986
5146	Magee, Sibyle		
		Kennon E. Magee	20 Nov. 1962
81184a	Magil, Anson J.		
		Linda Magil	28 May 1982
6096	Mahin, Dian Graves		
		Hilary D. Mahin	5 Aug. 1965
4173	Mahon, Marie		
		Everett Mahon	11 May 1955
2761	Main, Helen		
		Alfonso Main	19 Dec. 1944
8832a	Maley, Michael		
		Shannon Maley	13 Apr. 1988
8196a	Maloy, Mary Linda Smith		
		James Clayton Maloy	7 July 1981
5682	Mangham, George		
		Roberta Willson Mangham	19 May 1966
2746	Manley, John D. III		
		Elizabeth Y. Manley	5 Apr. 1945

Case	Plaintiff	Defendant	Date
88176a	Mann, Shelli Dianne		
		John Frederick Mann	16 Nov. 1988
84106a	Mansmith, Bonita		
		Donald Ray Mansmith	9 Nov. 1984
81169a	Marble, Shirley Ruth		
		Dale Ernest Marble	16 Oct. 1981
3343	Marburger, Nora H.		
		P. L. Marburger	8 Feb. 1949
5689	March, Baby Ray		
		Frankie Dou March	22 June 1966
6956	Marines, Alice Sifuentes		
		Saragoza Madrid Marines	1 Feb. 1978
3109	Marines, Jesus		
		Elvira Marines	17 Apr. 1947
8736a	Marino, Joseph Anthony		
		Sharon Lee Marino	8 June 1988
2464	Marion, Winifred B.		
		Judge Wilson Marion	11 Mar. 1941
78176a	Marks, Sally Lee		
		Richard Henry Marks	15 Feb. 1980
6193	Markwordt, Charles		
		Hazel Markwordt	15 May 1969
4252	Markwordt, Evelyn		
		Charles Markwordt	5 Sept. 1955
8697a	Marlele, Nettie S.		
		Dale E. Marlele	19 Dec. 1986
2986	Marlow, Edna J.		
		E. W. Marlow	5 June 1946
3198	Marlowe, Edna J.		
		E. W. Marlowe	11 Nov. 1947
87194a	Marmor, Avanelle Colleen		
		John William Marmor	7 Aug. 1988
5574	Marschall, Eldon		
		Dorothy M. Marschall	18 Jan 1966
6198	Marshall, Shirley Ann		
		Chas. David Marshall	24 May 1971
1631	Marshall, W. G.		
		Minnie Marshall	8 Oct. 1931
3057	Martin, A.		
		Isabell Martin	6 Nov. 1946
6039	Martin, Betty Jean		
		Harvey Clyde Martin	9 June 1968
82155	Martin, Donna B.		
		Homer V. Martin Jr.	22 Oct. 1982

Case	Plaintiff	Defendant	Date
4312	Martin, James I.		
		Geraldine L. Martin	5 June 1956
4939	Martin, Lydia L.		
		James I. Martin	10 Mar. 1961
3409	Martin, Mamie		
		Curtis Martin	18 July 1949
3026	Martin, Mamie F.		
		Curtis C. Martin	4 Sept. 1946
2243	Martin, Mary		
		Grady B. Martin	30 Sept. 1938
2772	Martin, Ola		
		Andrew Martin	19 Dec. 1944
83211a	Martin, Shirley Ann		
		David Alexander Martin	2 Dec. 1983
6423	Martin, Virgina N.		
		James C. Martin	26 May 1970
6102	Martinez, Amado A. Jr.		
		Socorra C. Martinez	20 Sept. 1968
2681	Martinez, Amelia		
		Marcelino Martinez	7 Dec. 1943
8742a	Martinez, Diana F.		
		Antonio V. Martinez	15 Jan. 1988
2886	Martinez, Gregoria		
		Willie Martinez	10 Dec. 1945
2804	Martinez, Leonoro		
		Ventura Martinez	8 June 1945
8382a	Martinez, Marilyn Lynn		
		Leo C. Martinez	16 Dec. 1983
80180a	Martinez, Ora Lee		
		Walter Arreola Martinez	7 Apr. 1981
8246a	Mason, Eugenia Lu Hill		
		John Earl Mason	21 July 1982
8565a	Mason, Mary Ann		
		Terry Lynn Mason	19 Dec. 1985
2910	Mason, Ruth Aline		
		Charles Robert Mason	22 Apr. 1946
4103	Massey, Andrew Raymond		
		Jewel Irene Massey	8 Sept. 1954
4931	Massey, Ben		
		Norma Leona Massey	20 Feb. 1961
6835	Massey, Bradford Clay		
		Penelope Gail Hunter Miller	
			23 May 1977

Case	Plaintiff	Defendant	Date
5758	Massey, Carol Jean		
		Wm. Henry Massey	2 Dec. 1966
1861	Massey, Dallas		
		Addie Lee Massey	2 Apr. 1934
5196	Massey, Dessie Irene		
		Andrew Raymond Massey	30 Apr. 1963
5457	Massey, Mordlene B.		
		Harold D. Massey	30 Apr. 1965
4704	Massey, Mordlene Belle		
		Harold Dean Massey	26 Feb. 1959
4247	Massey, Nancy Ella		
		Walter R. Massey	5 Sept. 1955
3847	Massey, William M.		
		Margaret L. Massey	15 Dec. 1952
8039a	Matheny, Hal Frank		
		Elizabeth Mc Millan Matheny	
			23 Dec. 1980
4705	Matheson, Martha E.		
		Dewey O'Daniel Matheson	2 Mar. 1959
5553	Matter, Charles G.		
		Ila Dean Matter	20 Nov. 1965
83152a	Matter, Crystal Michelle		
		Terry Jordon Matter	4 Oct. 1983
6173	Matthews, Dorothy Ann St. Clair		
		Henry Neal Matthews	21 Jan 1967
88244a	Matthews, Lorenzo George Jr.		
		Gwendolyn Clark Matthews	
			11 Jan. 1989
78127a	Matthews, Thos. Graham		
		Judy Matthews	20 Nov. 1979
80135a	Mathis, Sharon Lyn		
		Lawrence Gerald Mathis	11 Aug. 1980
5655	Maughn, Brenda Joyce		
		Andrew Jefferson Maughn	16 May 1966
6246	Maxwell, Bonnie C.		
		Charles R. Maxwell	22 July 1969
3161	Maxwell, Kitty West		
		Jas. W. Maxwell	14 Sept. 1947
6429	May, Dewey A.		
		Enola Pearl May	10 June 1970
2879	May, Ethel Margaret		
		Dewey A. May	13 Nov. 1945
3043	May, Ethel Lee		
		Dewey Allen May	25 Oct. 1946

Case	Plaintiff	Defendant	Date
84189a	May, William H.		
		Gretchen E. May	30 Aug. 1984
5035	Mayberry, Stella M.		
		Eddie Mayberry	13 May 1963
2065	Maynard, Ellen		
		W. F. Maynard	30 June 1937
3547	Mayo, Dean		
		Richard Mayo	19 May 1950
5732	Mays, Evelyn Inez		
		Robt. Paul Mays Jr.	9 Mar. 1967
78133a	McBride, Laura Mays		
		Ralph H. McBride	29 Mar. 1979
82175a	McBride, Stella M. R.		
		David A. McBride	5 Nov. 1982
5728	McCollum, Elma		
		Floyd McCollum	21 Sept. 1966
1800	McCarty, Hazel		
		Herbert McCarty	11 Oct. 1933
82188a	McClennahan, Claude Reed		
		Kelly Maureen	21 Jan. 1983
7881a	McClung, Barbara Jean		
		Jerry Lee McClung	26 Feb. 1979
82104a	McCoy, Cynthia Kathleen		
		Tommie Ray McCoy Jr.	16 Sept. 1980
88278a	McCracken, Bob Louis		
		Jewell Darlene McCracken	1 Mar. 1989
5292	McCray, C. W.		
		Martha Estell McCray	17 Feb. 1964
4731	McCray, Mary Jane		
		Harvey Lester McCray	28 Sept. 1959
89310a	McCray, Leonie B.		
		Ellis McCray	9 Jan. 1985
3886	McCullor, R. C.		
		Nancy McCullor	16 Dec. 1952
3468	McDade, L. A.		
		Iva Lorene McDade	12 Dec. 1949
2401	McDaniel, Dida		
		Frank McDaniel	28 Mar. 1940
8339a	McDaniel, Linda Fay		
		James Raymond McDaniel	25 May 1983
83101a	McDaniel Linda L.		
		Jack M. McDaniel	15 Jan. 1984
5929	McDaniel, Vickie		
		B. W. McDaniel	9 Sept. 1967

Case	Plaintiff	Defendant	Date
5647	McDonald, Audrey Maxine		
	James Ray McDonald		16 Mar. 1966
8311a	McDonald, Donald Lee		
	Faith Ellen McDonald		24 Mar. 1983
2492	McDonald, Mary M.		
	Chester R. McDonald		25 Mar. 1941
85279a	McElhannon, Thomas A.		
	Laura S. McElhannon		15 Apr. 1986
2641	McElrath, George		
	Zell McElrath		23 Mar. 1943
2975	McElroy, Daisy E.		
	George E. McElroy		3 May 1946
3704	McElroy, Ilse F.		
	Jim McElroy		10 Sept. 1951
5046	McGee, Harvey Clifton		
	Ellen Louise McGee		15 Jan. 1962
3455	McGee, Myrtle		
	Ira T. McGee		19 Apr. 1950
6085	McGehee, Willie Gene		
	Robert Brenda McGehee		15 July 1968
82265a	McGhee, Fay Nell		
	James Ernest McGhee		18 Nov. 1983
83176a	McGreevy, Patrick Charles		
	Wilma Joy McGreevy		14 Oct. 1983
5811	McGrew, Billy Ray		
	Fannie Catherine B. McGrew		
			23 Jan. 1967
7951a	McGrew, Billy Ray		
	Motoka Miza McGrew		30 May 1979
1929	McHoes, L. L.		
	Mary O. McHoes		24 Oct. 1935
4697	McKay, Barbara		
	Roy D. McKay		12 Feb. 1959
5458	McKay Roy D.		
	Bernadine McKay		22 Jan. 1965
1891	McIntosh, Dr. S. F.		
	Dorothy McIntosh		7 Oct. 1935
5182	McLaughlin, Virginia		
	James McLaughlin		11 Jan. 1963
4010	McLeod, Dwight E.		
	Helen L. McLeod		7 Dec. 1953
5157	McMaham, Craig A.		
	Karen McMahan		18 Oct. 1963

Case	Plaintiff	Defendant	Date
2801	McManus, Isabell		
		Robert McManus	5 Apr. 1945
1917	McMillan, Karin		
		W. M. McMillan	6 Oct. 1935
3471	McMillan, Mattie		
		W. M. McMillan	12 Dec. 1949
78158a	McNatt, Patricia P.		
		Shelton McNatt	29 Mar. 1979
1602	McNaughton, Bessie		
		Joe McNaughton	30 Mar. 1931
5865	McNeeley, Ethel		
		John F. McNeeley Jr.	6 June 1967
7862a	McNutt, Fred Emerson Jr.		
		Willa Reid McNutt	19 Oct. 1978
2812	McRae, Alexander		
		Theresa McRae	8 June 1945
3100	McRoy, Bonnie		
		Floyd McRoy	26 Mar. 1947
1715	McRoy, Floyd		
		Florence McRoy	4 Oct. 1932
2066	McRoy, Floyd		
		Willie Joe McRoy	10 Oct. 1936
2528	McRoy, Floyd		
		Thelma A. McRoy	20 Sept. 1941
4787	McRoy, Floyd		
		Bonnie McRoy	26 Oct. 1959
87234a	Meade, Robert L.		
		Gerladine J. Meade	5 Jan, 1987
83112a	Meade, Robert Lee		
		Geraldine Meade	29 Oct. 1984
79264a	Meadow, Philip Leroy		
		Mary Annette Chesser Meadow	
			25 Aug. 1980
2773	Medlock, Lewis		
		Jewel Medlock	19 Dec. 1944
8495a	Medrano, Claudia Olvitta		
		Balentino O. Medrano	8 June 1984
4756	Medrano, Eudivigen A.		
		David A. Medrano	4 Aug. 1959
5697	Medrano, Henry		
		Irma Medrano	16 Feb. 1967
4344	Medrano, Valentino		
		Patsy Medrano	13 Aug. 1956

Case	Plaintiff	Defendant	Date
3357	Medcalf, Elizabeth E.		
	Horace C. Medcalf		7 Feb. 1949
88060a	Meek, Carl Donald		
	Margaret Ann Meek		23 Feb. 1989
7882a	Meek, Curtis Lee		
	Yen Ming Meek		20 Dec. 1978
5780	Meek, Rosa Lea		
	Carl D. Meek		30 Mar. 1967
85300a	Meinecke, Steven L.		
	Brenda E. Garrett Horton Meinecke		31 July 1986
84212a	Mejia, Cordova Felix		
	Gloria Gomez Mejia		21 Nov. 1984
84144a	Melton, Deliaiah Darlene		
	Richard Louis Melton		16 Aug. 1984
2548	Menchaca, F. R.		
	Savino Menchaca		16 Mar. 1942
8127a	Menchaca, Jesse V.		
	Mary Esther Menchaca		21 Oct. 1981
81146a	Menchaca, Melinda		
	Edward Menchaca		17 Sept. 1981
4445	Mendoza, Beatrice		
	Ben Mendoza		3 June 1057
3582	Mendoza, Medardo		
	Binegra G. S Mendoza		15 Nov. 1950
2515	Menges, Annie Mae		
	Louis Menges		16 Dec. 1941
83170a	Menn, Francisca Gonzales		
	Stephen Menn		16 Dec. 1983
7046	Menn, Mary R.		
	Hugo F. Menn		28 Aug. 1978
82249a	Mercer, Billy R.		
	Velma J. Mercer		21 Jan. 1983
81170a	Mercer, James Ray		
	Corina Flo Mercer		23 Nov. 1981
4113	Meredith, Audrey		
	William R. Meredith		7 Sept. 1954
1909	Merrill, Amy		
	Virgil Merrill		2 Apr. 1935
1875	Merritt, A. E.		
	Katherine J. Merritt		9 Oct. 1934

81132a Merritt, Cecil Owen II
            Bridget Langdale Merritt
                                    24 Aug. 1981
3252   Merritt, Frances Doyle
            Arvil Merritt   14 June 1948
5319   Messer, Fred Wayne
            Brenda Jean Messer   17 Apr. 1964
3315   Messick, Winona
            Bryan Messick   25 Oct. 1948
5058   Metheny, Sharon
            Hal Matheny   12 Mar. 1962
86179a Methvon, Parker Burette
            Patricia Elaine Methvon 5 Sept, 1986
2333   Metzger, Essie Mae
            L. A. Metzger   19 Sept. 1939
121   Meyer, Edith
            R. C. Meyer Jr.   4 Mar. 1970
4550   Meyer, Fred A.
            Mary E. Meyer   12 Nov. 1958
2268   Meyer, Selma
            Louis Meyer   6 Mar. 1939
5714   Meyners, Elizabeth Ann
            Alfred Lance Meyners Sr.
                                    15 Aug. 1966
4394   Michael, Lucille
            John Michael   19 Oct. 1956
4045   Michon, Benj. Franklin
            Lucille Michon   26 July 1954
2647   Middlebrook, Model
            Hosa F. Middlebrook   6 Sept. 1943
8373a   Middleton, Lela Mary
            William Robert Middleton Jr.
                                    10 June 1983
84284a Middleton, Randall Allan
            Donna Janise Middleton 27 Dec. 1984
3047   Miears, J. D.
            Edna Miears   25 Oct. 1946
6111   Miears, Jeanetta F.
            Harold Miears   8 Nov. 1968
1896   Miears, Millie
            Clyde H. Miears   26 Oct. 1934
2100   Miears, Millie E.
            Clyde Miears   19 Apr. 1937

Case	Plaintiff	Defendant	Date
3409	Mika, John J.		
		Helen V. Mika	7 Sept. 1949
8128a	Mikeska, Frank John		
		Betty Eugene Clark Mikeska	6 Aug. 1981
78142a	Milholland, Jay G.		
		Viola M. Milholland	14 Feb. 1979
6814	Miller, Bobbie Sue Ann		
		Ray Buford Miller	12 May 1977
8450a	Miller, Karen Virginia		
		Joe Davis Miller	3 May 1984
6222	Miller, Linda Kay		
		Roy Lee Miller	8 May 1969
5705	Miller, Marion Ruth		
		E. Todd Miller	8 Dec. 1966
3363	Miller, Dr. R. E. L.		
		Annie L. Miller	14 Mar. 1949
84301a	Miller, Ronald Gene		
		Joyce Nell Miller	27 Dec. 1984
826a	Miller, Shirley Jane		
		Harold John Miller	7 Apr. 1982
88142a	Miller, Valerie May		
		Ronald James Miller	27 Mar. 1989
79197a	Miller, Wallace V.		
		Margaret G. Miller	20 Dec. 1979
5315	Miller, Winnie Doris		
		Jess G. Miller	26 Mar. 1964
1659	Mills, Ella		
		J. C. Mills	29 Mar. 1932
1665	Mills, Ella		
		J. C. Mills	24 Oct. 1931
5849	Mills, Irene		
		Herman Lewis Mills	18 May 1967
4583	Mills, Mary Anne		
		Joseph Glenn Mills	29 Nov. 1958
3489	Miner, Mary		
		Thomas E. Miner	6 Feb. 1950
84269a	Mirelis, Serapia C. Moreno		
		Jesse Mirelis	21 Nov. 1984
3701	Mitchell, J. D.		
		Myrtle Mitchell	5 Sept. 1951
5890	Mitchell, Leroy		
		Beverly Ann Mitchell	28 June 1967

Case	Plaintiff	Defendant	Date
3407	Mitchell, Winnie		
		J. D. Mitchell	18 July 1949
2474	Mittank, Ervin A.		
		Rose Marie Mittank	11 Mar. 1941
5898	Mixon, Shirley Bobbie		
		Perry Van Mixon	2 Aug. 1967
79199a	Modgling, Carol Lynn		
		Kenneth Glen Modgling	29 Aug. 1980
5566	Modgling, Nahum Bert		
		Norma Jean Modgling	22 Dec. 1965
4150	Moekle, Johanna M.		
		Damon Carol Moekle	22 Dec. 1954
7023	Moller, Fay H.		
		B. Weems Moller	18 May 1978
8047a	Moncus, Jacqueline Annette		
		Wm. Stephen Moncus	25 Apr. 1980
87227a	Mongello, Cynthia Ann		
		Harry Vincent Mongello Jr.	7 Apr. 1988
79288a	Monk, Charles Robert		
		Loretta Dee Monk	26 Feb. 1980
8166a	Monson, Scott Bruce		
		Veronica Kay Monson	28 June 1982
3742	Montana, Esther Romona		
		Jose Montana	4 Feb. 1952
2212	Montez, Felepe		
		Manuel Montez	21 Sept. 1938
1697	Montgomery, Katherine		
		Wm. N. Montgomery	12 Apr. 1932
85215a	Montoya, Betty Jo		
		Keith Arthur Montoya	15 Aug. 1986
2950	Moody, Mary G. M.		
		W. L. Moody IV	30 May 1946
84333a	Moore, Allan Roy		
		Darlene P. Moore	6 Mar. 1985
8540a	Moore, Christine Henderson		
		Thomas J. Moore	23 May 1985
4958	Moore, Hertha Biermann		
		Walter Freeman Moore	10 Mar. 1961
6083	Moore, James Franklin		
		Linda Carmen Moore	25 June 1968
2493	Moore, Jas. J.		
		A. Leone H. Moore	9 Mar. 1942

Case	Plaintiff	Defendant	Date
2478	Moore, Jno. J.		
		Mary Agnes Moore	11 Mar. 1941
8057a	Moore, Katie Catheline		
		Lester Lee Moore	20 June 1980
6963	Moore, Leo		
		Christine Moore	19 Jan. 1978
2506	Moore, Melissa Jane		
		Charles A. Moore	9 Mar. 1942
1837	Moore, Ora Mae		
		Charles A. Moore	27 Mar. 1934
6055	Moore, Shirley N.		
		Raymond Riley Moore	21 Aug. 1968
1974	Moore, Mrs. Tom K.		
		Tom K. Moore	26 Apr. 1935
3146	Moore, Verna		
		Oriel W. Moore	10 June 1947
3051	Moore, Vincent B.		
		Irma Lee Moore	6 Nov. 1946
3794	Moose, Ann Hubble		
		Benj. (Bennie) Moose	12 May 1953
2601	Moose, Benjamin F.		
		Bertha Mae Moose	8 Oct. 1942
2093	Moose, Thyrza		
		Alvin Moose	31 Mar. 1937
2276	Morales, Antonio		
		Eucebia Morales	7 Mar. 1939
2439	Morales, Antonio		
		Lila Morales	11 Mar. 1941
5639	Moran, Kathryn Lofters		
		Joseph J. Moran	25 Feb. 1966
3643	Moreau, Edward C.		
		Marion Wanda Moreau	19 May 1951
4784	Moreau, Edward C.		
		Elizabeth Moreau	12 Jan. 1960
5701	Moreno, David C.		
		Yolanda Garza Moreno	15 Aug. 1966
6235	Moreno, Jesusa Sandoval		
		Guadalupe Moreno	17 July 1970
2147	Morgan, Mack		
		Mollie Morgan	21 Sept. 1937
3625	Morgan, William J.		
		Janet M. Morgan	23 Apr. 1951
3750	Morin, Ramon		
		Refugia Marin	14 July 1953

Case	Plaintiff	Defendant	Date
84170a	Morocco, Frank Domenia Jr.		
		Linda Darlene Morocco	16 Aug. 1984
2721	Morris, Charles E.		
		Bertha Morris	9 June 1944
79129a	Morris, David Jefferson		
		Rosemary Russell Morris	18 Jan. 1980
1729	Morris, Katie		
		T. E. Morris	4 Oct. 1932
3761	Morris, Jessie		
		W. J. Morris	4 Feb. 1952
8640a	Morris, Rodney Melvin		
		Patricia N. V. Morris	5 Apr. 1986
4199	Morris, W. J.		
		Agnes Morris	11 May 1955
1876	Morrison, Clara		
		Clarence Morrison	24 Oct. 1934
2430	Morrison, Clara		
		Clarence Morrison	17 Sept. 1940
2389	Morrison, J. M.		
		Emma Morrison	19 Mar. 1940
7855a	Morriss, Deborah		
		Gordon Sproul Morriss	28 Feb. 1980
1794	Morrow, Bernice		
		Ike Morrow	19 Oct. 1933
5757	Mosby, Andrea Eliz.		
		William Henry Mosby	10 Dec. 1966
4434	Moseley, Jean		
		L. S. Moseley	3 June 1957
87100a	Moss, Marvin Walter		
		Pamela Nell Moss	28 Sept. 1987
83124a	Mouton, Albert J.		
		Gladys Lucille Mouton	3 Aug. 1983
8745a	Mueller, Steve Allen		
		Patricia Ann Mueler	2 Dec. 1987
5790	Mullins, Doris Sue		
		Kenneth David Mullins	8 Dec. 1977
8796a	Mulson, Mabel Josephine		
		Harvey Leuis Mulson	8 July 1987
79195a	Mumme, Alfred E.		
		Margaret Ann Mimme	25 Jan. 1980
4347	Mund, Katherine		
		Bennie F. Mund	6 Aug. 1956
85223a	Munoz, Alice Benjamin		
		Martin Ramirez Munoz	22 Oct. 1985

Case	Plaintiff	Defendant	Date
87270a	Murphy, Barbara Lee		
		Timothy Gerard Murphy	5 May 1988
3147	Murphy, Clarence		
		Dorothy Murphy	5 Aug. 1947
86114a	Murphy, Joyce Lynn		
		Carl Hughes Murphy	19 June 1986
1905	Murphy, Ruth		
		Clarence Murphy	2 Apr. 1935
3874	Murray, Carolyn S.		
		James Howard Murray	10 Feb. 1953
4261	Murray, Nancy Jane		
		James H. Myrray	10 Oct. 1955
4545	Muse, Howard C.		
		Louise R. Muse	8 Sept. 1958
8236a	Myers, Fred A.		
		Judith G. Myers	28 May 1982
8064a	Myers, Kathryn Elaine		
		Richard R. Myers	29 Sept. 1980

N

Case	Plaintiff	Defendant	Date
86222a	Nabors, Jodie Petey		
		James McLaughlin Nabors Jr.	
			5 Nov. 1986
1714	Nalls, Blanche		
		F. E. Nalls	6 Oct. 1932
2813	Nalls, Vina Pearl		
		Floyd E. Nalls	8 June 1945
1888	Nance, A. E.		
		Agnes K. Nance	26 Oct. 1934
1782	Nanny, Lula		
		Charles L. Nanny	28 Oct. 1933
1971	Naper, Elmer E.		
		Nellie M. Naper	25 Oct. 1935
3633	Nash, Estelle		
		Hilory Nash	4 Sept. 1951
3965	Nash, Frances Fullwood		
		Hilory Nash	8 Sept. 1953
87187a	Nash, Yvonne Rachel		
		James Marvin Nash III	3 Aug. 1988
3391	Neagle, Veda		
		Marlin Neagle	23 May 1949

Case	Plaintiff	Defendant	Date
5357	Neal Bill Junior		
		Melba Faye Neal	6 June 1964
2564	Neal, Clay		
		Edna Neal	2 Jan. 1942
84311a	Neal, Doreen Rita		
		Anthony Elijah Neal	24 Apr. 1985
79270a	Neal, Hannah Mae		
		Anthony Elijah Neal	10 Dec. 1980
3307	Neal, Madge Leola		
		Merrill F. Neal	22 Nov. 1948
4194	Nealis, Lillie		
		Floyd Nealis	11 May 1955
2699	Neff, Myrel		
		W. V. Neff	9 June 1944
2394	Neidecken, Patty		
		C. S. Neidecken	20 Mar. 1940
3799	Nelms, Eliz. Williams		
		Albert Llewellyn Nelms Jr.	
			21 May 1952
3350	Nelson, Ben		
		Saretta Nelson	7 Feb. 1949
38	Nelson, E. C.		
		P. M. Nelson	29 Nov. 1860
3211	Nelson, Florence		
		George Nelson	16 Dec. 1947
3590	Nelson, June Jerney		
		Frank Nelson	5 Sept. 1951
5258	Nelson, Pauline Crenshaw		
		Jack L. Nelson	19 Oct. 1963
1858	Nentwig, Joe Jerry		
		Hazel Nentwig	16 Apr. 1934
4153	Nesby, Naomi Lewis		
		Preston Nesby	9 Feb. 1955
80149a	Neutze, Robert		
		Margie Louise Neutze	28 Oct. 1980
16	New, Carolyn		
		George New	18 Nov. 1858
4230	Newbury, Clinton J.		
		Bonny J. Newbury	12 Aug. 1955
1735	Newcomer, Alice B.		
		J. A. Newcomer	14 Oct. 1932
4068	Newell, Louis E.		
		Mary Ann Newell	1 June 1954

Case	Plaintiff / Defendant	Date
3062	Newman, Vernell Johnnie H. Newman	2 Jan. 1947
3207	Newton, Myrtle Mitchell J. K. Newton	15 Dec. 1947
4296	Nichols, Gerald Thomas Ruth Eliz. Nichols	19 Apr. 1956
3275	Nichols, Jean Ware Smith E. Nichols	29 July 1948
3802	Nichols, Leatha Mae Lyle Leslie Nichols	23 May 1952
1944	Nichols, Mamie Ethel Charles D. Nichols	8 Oct. 1935
2954	Nichols, Mamie Lou Lyle L. Nichols	22 Apr. 1946
3070	Nichols, Margaret J. J. Nichols	3 Feb. 1947
2162	Nichols, Mary Elvis Nichols	28 Mar. 1938
85198a	Nichols Michael Louise Cranz Larry Nichols	14 Nov. 1986
4964	Nichols, Minnie Hugh Nichols	15 May 1961
3439	Nichols, Vida Mae Lyle Leslie Nichols	12 Dec. 1949
6319	Nichols, Wanda Everett Earl Nichols	31 Dec. 1969
3151	Nichols, Willie B. Agnes Nichols	5 July 1947
3603	Nipper, Blanch G. Henry Burr Nipper	30 Jan. 1951
2794	Nipps, Nannie J. J. F. Nipps	5 Apr. 1945
5500	Nixon, Sondra Dennie Randal Nixon	9 July 1965
8229a	Noble, Joanna Blackwell Calvin E. Noble	18 June 1982
1962	Noll, Stella Henry Noll	23 Oct. 1935
3194	Norman, Marie William F. Norman	20 Dec. 1948
2987	Norman, W. F. Marjory Louise Norman	20 June 1946
83297a	Norris, James David Carline Norris	23 Mar. 1984

Case	Plaintiff	Defendant	Date
3252	Norris, Lawrence E.		
		Barbara Lawrence	10 Sept. 1948
84188a	Norris, Melinda Nell		
		Walter Warren Norris	12 Oct. 1984
87271a	North, Suzanne L.		
		Lee Frank North	3 Aug. 1988
1833	Northrup, J. Robert		
		Rosalie Northrup	29 Mar. 1934
5784	Norton, Charles S.		
		Lola Norton	2 Dec. 1966
5899	Norton, Charles Stewart		
		Agnes Rosie Norton	6 Sept, 1967
5118	Novasad, Betty Louise		
		Charles Novasad	23 July 1962
81237a	Nowlin, Charles A.		
		Myrtle O. Nowlin	4 Feb. 1982
3145	Nowlin, Ethel		
		R. B. Nowlin	13 June 1947
4961	Nugent, Doris Marie		
		Victor John Nugent	11 Mar. 1961
84279a	Nunn, Natalee B.		
		Willaim A. Nunn	27 Dec. 1984
86166a	Nurse, Francis V.		
		America Malinda Nurse	16 Mar. 1987
4486	Nuttall, Dovie		
		Aylmer (Bobbie) Nuttall	13 Aug. 1957
2078	Nyc, F. F.		
		Maude Ruth Nyc	22 Oct. 1936

O

Case	Plaintiff	Defendant	Date
3560	Oates, Inez C.		
		Luther R. Oates	5 Sept. 1950
88223a	O'Brien, Viegnia Marie		
		Raymond Hamilton O'Brien	
			24 May 1989
2240	O'Bryant, Alma Lee		
		George J. O'Bryant	20 Sept. 1938
2038	O'Bryant, Ethel		
		L. M. O'Bryant	7 Oct. 1936
6265	O'Conner, Janette Allen		
		Charles Joseph O'Conner	28 July 1969

Case	Plaintiff	Defendant	Date
7947a	O'Dell, David Melton Sr.		
		Barbara Lynn O'Dell	20 June 1979
87122a	O'Dell, Carolyn Lee		
		David Melton O'Dell	17 Aug. 1987
5988	Oestreich, Esther E.		
		Lewis H. Oestreich	24 Jan. 1968
8293a	Ogden, Bobbie Ann		
		Willie Eugene Ogdon	5 Nov. 1982
84132a	Ogden, Susan Louise		
		Willie Eugene Ogden	26 July 1984
2435	Oldham, Essie M.		
		Odis W. Oldham	12 Mar. 1941
8230a	Olivares, Candido Herrera		
		Sandra B. Olivares	28 May 1982
2915	Olivarez, Martha P.		
		Juan S. Olivarez	25 Feb. 1946
5123	Oman, Viola		
		Sammie Arthur Oman	13 Aug. 1962
80264a	Ontivaros, Paula G.		
		Fructuoca A. Ontivaros	31 July 1981
4628	Ontiveros, Ramona		
		Pablo Ontiveros	13 Oct. 1958
86131a	Ordza, Janie		
		Calixto Juan Ordza	1 July 1986
8488a	O'Rear, James B.		
		Mary Lou O'Rear	12 July 1984
1873	Orr, Pearl		
		W. S. Orr	10 Oct. 1934
3573	Orsack, Peggy Joy		
		Ben Orsack	17 Mar. 1951
4796	Ortega, Frank		
		Maria Louisa Ortega	9 Dec. 1959
2303	Ortega, Santos F.		
		Frank Ortega	29 Mar. 1939
3256	Osborne, La Verne		
		Charles Carroll Osborne	
			26 June 1950
7030	Ostenson, David Lee		
		Gloria Hope Ostenson	16 June 1978
8177a	Ott, Linda Sue		
		Clifton Wayne Ott	13 Nov. 1981
81202a	Ottmers, Rhonda Particia		
		Gary Lee Ottmers	24 Nov. 1981

Case	Plaintiff	Defendant	Date
3034	Oubre, Dorothy		
		Alvie Oubre	4 Sept. 1946
6154	Owen, Alice May		
		Horace E. Owen	6 Jan, 1969
1606	Owen, R. E.		
		Willie S. Owen	1 Apr. 1931
1660	Owen, Ruby		
		Ross Owen	12 Oct. 1931
1708	Owens, Leo		
		Lora Owens	20 Apr. 1932
4636	Owens, Milton T.		
		Pearl Owens	8 Dec. 1958
1797	Owens, Viola		
		Milton Owens	13 Oct. 1933
2322	Ozuna, Horace		
		Margaret Ozuna	25 Apr. 1939
2418	Ozuna, Phillip		
		Madaline Ozuna	16 Sept. 1941
4594	Ozuna, Yrbano		
		Florinda Ozuna	31 Oct. 1958

P

Case	Plaintiff	Defendant	Date
79160a	Pace, Winfield Jennings		
		Vera Oleta Pace	19 Nov. 1979
4855	Pachall, Catherine		
		Richard A. Pachall	30 Apr. 1960
4730	Page, Betty Lou		
		W. E. Page	21 Apr. 1959
2567	Page, J. E.		
		Velma Page	23 Mar. 1942
2694	Page, Jewel		
		J. E. Page	28 Mar. 1944
3368	Page, Leatha Mae		
		Charley J. Page	14 Mar. 1949
5680	Page, Melba Jean		
		William E. Page	7 July 1966
3098	Page, Ruby Henly		
		Clarence Page	14 Apr. 1947
4886	Page, Sue H.		
		W. E. Page	17 Aug. 1960
4649	Paine, Barbara Ann		
		Robert Neal Paine	14 Oct. 1958

Case	Plaintiff	Defendant	Date
5062	Paine, Robert		
		Barbara Ann Paine	11 Jan. 1963
5831	Paine, Vivian Elizabeth		
		Billy Wayne Paine Sr.	7 Mar. 1967
84217a	Paiz, Amalia		
		Johnny O. Paiz	12 Oct. 1984
6040	Pakkila, Helen K.		
		Andrew J. Pakkila	20 May 1968
858a	Palm, Kirsten Ingeberg		
		Jan Hendirck Palm	20 Sept, 1985
806a	Paris, Rickey Ned		
		Chari Ann Paris	31 Oct. 1980
793a	Paris, Sherron K.		
		Rickey Ned Paris	2 May 1979
4722	Parker, Dorothy		
		Dubois Parker	14 Sept. 1959
4804	Parker, Eva D. Johnston		
		Clayton Clyde Parker	14 Dec. 1959
2663	Parker, John Neal		
		Mabel M. Parker	8 June 1943
81208a	Parker, May Frances		
		Douglas Lambert Parker	7 June 1982
4302	Parker, Vera Irene		
		Clayton C. Parker	27 Mar. 1956
4615	Parker, Wanda June		
		Clayton C. Parker	2 June 1958
4543	Parks, Alice		
		William Parks	13 Dec. 1957
4551	Parks, Hattie Baldwin		
		Irvin Parks	20 Dec. 1957
2934	Parks, Robert Lee		
		Mildred E. Parks	5 Mar. 1946
4385	Parmelee, Barbara		
		Clyde D. Parmelee	5 Oct. 1956
3135	Parr, Louise		
		Roland Parr	9 June 1947
8184a	Parrish, Beverly Ann		
		Harry A. Parrish	10 Sept. 1981
6856	Parry, Frances Jo Casey		
		William Allan Parry III	14 July 1977
5879	Parry, William Allan		
		Romaona Parry	15 June 1967
5771	Pate, Barbare Allyn		
		Clarence Pate	2 Dec. 1966

Case	Plaintiff	Defendant	Date
5135	Patterson, Mae Louise Schreiner		
		John C. Patterson	7 Sept. 1962
80206a	Patterson, William R.		
		Afton B. Patterson	19 Dec. 1980
84176a	Patton, Sarah Ann		
		Hugh Patton	11 July 1985
2253	Paul, Meta		
		H. T. Paul	3 Oct. 1938
838a	Paul, Sandra		
		Samuel Ray Paul	15 Sept. 1983
3517	Pauley, Russell		
		Medora B. Pauley	19 May 1950
6289	Paxton, Claire M.		
		Lloyd Paxton	29 Aug. 1969
6950	Payne, Jo Ann		
		Charles Payne Jr.	19 Dec. 1977
2827	Pearce, Virginia M.		
		Rodney B. Pearce	16 July 1945
6216	Pearson, Bobbie Jane		
		Leroy Pearson	1 Sept. 1972
81204a	Pearson, David C.		
		Robbin Annette Pearson	17 Dec. 1981
3322	Pearson, Dolores		
		L. F. Pearson	22 Nov. 1948
4700	Pearson, Fred		
		Rose Pearson	2 Mar. 1959
85226a	Pearson, Hubert Wm.		
		Judy Carol Pearson	19 Dec. 1985
3615	Peavler, Ruth		
		Charley W. Peavler	18 Jan. 1952
5192	Peck, Elgin W.		
		Margaret Peck	23 Apr. 1963
85139a	Penney, Barbara J.		
		Edwin G. Penney	30 Apr. 1986
2920	Pepper, Ella		
		Austin Pepper	5 June 1946
2379	Perez, A. DeLa Cruz		
		Alfonso Perez	5 Mar. 1940
81150a	Perez, Elsa Casrillo		
		Benito Rivas Perez	9 Feb. 1982
1819	Perez, Ernesto		
		Jobila Perez	30 Mar. 1934
84364a	Perhamus, Richard Mark		
		Sally Ann Perhamus 3	6 Mar. 1985

Case	Plaintiff	Defendant	Date
2254	Perkins, Allie		
		Charles H. Perkins	20 Mar. 1939
8318a	Perkins, Cheryl Ann		
		Stephen Dean Mark Perkins	
			5 May 1983
3316	Perkins, Eleanor S.		
		Ralph I. Perkins	20 Dec. 1948
2926	Perner, Charlie		
		Ernestine Perner	5 Mar. 1946
3911	Perner, Hubert		
		Bonnie Jean Perner	13 Apr. 1953
6516	Peters, Donald B.		
		Eleanor Peters	7 Feb. 1972
5543	Peterson, Annie B.		
		Larry L. Peterson	24 July 1965
3265	Peterson, Hal		
		Audrey R. Peterson	10 Mar. 1949
3903	Peterson, Mirl B.		
		Orene A. Peterson	2 Feb. 1953
4736	Peterson, Mirl B.		
		Arlice O. Peterson	20 June 1959
6412	Peterson, Sue H.		
		George Gray Peterson	4 Sept, 1970
4926	Petley, Lynnie C.		
		George Edward Petley	23 May 1961
799a	Petmecky, Elvira M.		
		John P. Petmecky	4 Apr. 1979
4435	Pettit, E. R.		
		Bernice Pettit	30 Sept. 1957
8166a	Petitt, John W.		
		Loretta Pettit	25 June 1981
4132	Pettit, Velma		
		E. R. Pettit	20 Dec. 1954
3669	Pfeuffer, Ada		
		John Pfeuffer	27 Sept. 1951
2907	Pfeuffer, Lawrence L.		
		Mildred DeLois Pfeuffer	25 Feb. 1946
4386	Pfeuffer, Mary Lou		
		Lawrence Pfeuffer	14 Dec. 1956
8089a	Pfeuffer, Rugy Jewell		
		Raymond Leavell Pfeuffer	
			26 June 1980
2766	Pfeuffer, Zula Mae		
		Lawrence Pfeuffer	19 Dec. 1944

Case	Plaintiff	Defendant	Date
85199a	Phelps, Merle		
	Rachel Jane Boots Phelps		21 Nov. 1985
6318	Phillips, Charlotte		
	Thomas Ray Phillips		27 Jan. 1970
1654	Phillips, T. J.		
	Bernice Phillips		16 Oct. 1931
4101	Pieper, Henry Jr.		
	Annie Lee Pieper		26 July 1954
5083	Pieper, Henry Jr.		
	Mae Pieper		12 Mar. 1962
5265	Pierce, James M.		
	Betty Jean Pierce		19 Oct. 1963
5312	Pierce, Janice		
	Franklin C. Pierce Jr.		22 Dec. 1965
85259a	Pike, Saralen Elaine		
	John Austin Pike		24 Mar. 1986
80176a	Pilgram, Barbara Johnson		
	Joe Wayne Pilgram		20 Oct. 1980
1752	Pillow, Ruby		
	Clyde Lee Pillow		28 Mar. 1933
1801	Pitman, W. G.		
	Alletta Pitman		2 Apr. 1934
4413	Plant, Lou Lisa		
	Lester Plant		17 Dec. 1956
8360a	Plumly, Richard Fredericks		
	Pamela Anna Vlaskel Plumly		28 Mar. 1985
80283a	Plummer, Janet Rae		
	Willam Alexander Plummer III		19 Sept. 1981
8490a	Plummer, Sharon Marie		
	Gregory Allen Plummer		21 June 1984
2916	Ply, Green D.		
	Sadie Mae Ply		25 Feb. 1946
81245a	Poehler, Patsy Cleone		
	Phillip O'Neal Poehler		29 Jan. 1982
7012	Poenisch, Ernest M. Jr.		
	Lillian S. Poenisch		21 Sept. 1979
5373	Poindexter, Patricia Elaine		
	John R. Poindexter		4 Aug. 1964
4128	Pollack, Mary F.		
	Clinton A. Pollack		11 May 1955

Case	Plaintiff	Defendant	Date
85132a	Pollock, Jerome George Jr.	Doris Marie Carraleo Moody Pollock	28 Aug. 1985
4104	Pooler, Orvis John	Ella Mae Pooler	11 May 1955
4330	Poore, H. H. aka William A.	Ermeld Hohikounalani Poore	4 June 1956
6249	Poorman, Ruth E. M.	Van S. Poorman	29 May 1971
79215a	Pope, Orville Ray	Judith Kay Pope	15 Feb. 1980
4414	Pope, Ruby Ella	H. C. Pope	17 Dec. 1956
2833	Porch, Amy	Luther Porch	16 July 1945
3537	Porter, Elmer	Gladys Porter	28 Nov. 1950
4185	Porter, Helen L.	Alfred D. Porter	11 May 1955
5145	Porter, Zell G.	Lucille Cooper Porter	22 Dec. 1962
3795	Posey, Clarice Faye	E. Daniel Posey	2 Sept. 1952
85303a	Pospisil, Douglas R.	Diane Pospisil	23 Jan. 1986
5902	Poteet, Bonnie Jean	Edwin Layne Poteet	28 Aug. 1967
5345	Pothoff, Sherrilyn Shaw	Terry G. Pothoff	9 June 1964
80217a	Potter, Angeline Kay	Clarence Pellington Potter	8 Jan. 1981
84187a	Potts, Claudette Marie	Gregory Potts	30 Aug. 1984
4322	Powell, Angie	Sam A. Powell	8 Oct. 1956
3715	Powell, Herschel B.	Dorothy Lee Powell	19 Oct. 1951
8290a	Powell, Russell Allan	Lisa Ann Powell	30 Aug. 1982
2456	Power, Bertha	W. C. Power	29 Oct. 1940

Case	Plaintiff	Defendant	Date
2468	Power, Bertram		
		Angela Power	10 Mar. 1941
80287a	Power, Wesley Canfield		
		Hilda Crotez Power	5 Mar. 1981
3922	Prentice, Gloria Jeanette		
		James Gordon Prentice	13 Apr. 1953
8069a	Pressler, Rodney Joe		
		Patricia Jean Pressler	12 June 1980
2887	Price, Annie Low		
		George Green Price	9 Jan. 1945
8673a	Price, Bobby Jess		
		Marilyn W. Price	13 May 1986
3014	Price, Eileen		
		Jno. R. Price	24 Oct. 1946
2976	Price, Janie		
		Le Roy Price	25 Oct. 1946
3493	Prickle, Lillian		
		Ausie Prickle	19 Apr. 1950
8527a	Priour, Dolly Castle		
		Harlon Larry Priour	19 Dec. 1985
83239a	Priour, Gary Dale		
		Melodie Sayger Priour	24 Feb. 1984
81143a	Priour, John Thomas		
		Nancy Lee Priour	3 Sept. 1981
4827	Pritchett, V. E.		
		Alma K. Pritchett	5 Feb. 1960
79220a	Pruitt, Dora Louise		
		Ronnie Gale Pruitt Sr.	5 2 Jan. 1980
4262	Pruneda, Emma		
		Johnny Pruneda	10 Oct. 1955
3881	Pruneda, Jesus		
		Felipa Pruneda	15 Dec. 1952
4675	Pruneda, Rebecca		
		Amador Pruneda	12 Jan. 1959
5791	Puckett, Sam L.		
		Myara Jean Puckett	8 Dec. 1966
8529a	Pumphrey, Dorothy Barrett		
		Russell Ellis Pumphrey	25 June 1985
3076	Pumphrey, Joe M.		
		Lucien T. Pumphrey	3 Feb. 1947

Q

Case	Plaintiff	Defendant	Date

Case	Plaintiff / Defendant	Date
2841	Rabalois, Leonore Francois Rabalois	4 Sept. 1945
801a	Raborn, Barbara Hutchins James Jesse Raborn	16 Apr. 1980
2772	Raigorodsky, Edith M. Paul M. Raigorodsky	19 Dec. 1944
82105a	Rains, Eva Dee Leo Winfred Rains	12 Aug. 1982
7964a	Rainwater, Cliffa Jean Mickey Lynn Rainwater	15 June 1979
5622	Rainwater, Larry Ray Beverly Lynn Rainwater	31 Jan. 1966
6372	Rainwater, Nydia Jane Larry Ray Rainwater	18 Sept. 1970
86203a	Rames, Lorenzo Campeon Betty Ann Obiedo Rames	15 Oct. 1986
80163a	Ramirez, Alice Sufuentes Ramon Fabro Ramirez	16 Jan. 1981
81125a	Ramirez, Angelina Arturo Ramirez Sr.	30 Mar. 1982
5860	Ramirez, Basilia Alfredo Ramirez Jr.	20 Dec. 1967
2057	Ramirez, Blas Louisa Ramirez	7 Oct. 1936
2585	Ramirez, Gonzalo Maria Ramirez	3 Apr. 1942
87219a	Ramirez, Simon P. Jr. Hollie Jo Malsbury Ramirez	17 Feb. 1988
83147a	Ramsey, Mary Jean John Thos. Ramsey	15 Sept. 1983
2642	Ramos, Antonio N. Augustine R. Ramos	2 Apr. 1943
5513	Ramos, Martha Joe Ramos	12 July 1965
86273a	Ramos, Virginia Brondo Juan F. Ramos	14 July 1987
4909	Ramsour, Rose Kenneth Ramsour	23 Nov. 1960
86190a	Randall, Randall Lee Sylbia Pena Randall	31 Oct. 1986

Case	Plaintiff	Defendant	Date
8597a	Randall, Rolinda Jeanne		
		Clarence B. Randall Jr.	26 Sept. 1985
3939	Ranger, Gladys Jacob		
		Raymond Newton Ranger	7 Dec. 1953
4937	Ransleben, Eliz. Ann		
		Karl A. Ranseleben	15 Apr. 1961
2409	Ransom, Edna May		
		King R. Ransom	17 Sept. 1940
4059	Ransom, Lula Belle		
		Joe Kurt Ransom	8 Sept. 1954
86123a	Rathke, Harry Arnold		
		Evelyn Rathke	29 July 1986
6202	Rathke, Joyce A.		
		Calvin Rathke	13 Aug. 1969
83181a	Ratliff, Frances Elaine		
		Wayne Douglas Ratliff	14 Oct. 1983
2298	Rauch, Eleanor Burrer		
2299	Oscar Robt. Rauch		25 Apr. 1939
5583	Raute, George		
		Virginia Raute	21 Jan. 1966
2664	Ray, Allyne		
		James E. Ray	26 July 1943
4114	Rayburn, Avian F.		
		J. C. Rayburn	9 Sept. 1954
4484	Rayburn, Avain F.		
		J. C. Rayburn	11 July 1957
79122a	Rayes, Sue Ann		
		Alvin Allen Rayes	23 Aug. 1979
6631	Raymer, Gus		
		Loys Carver Raymer	25 Mar. 1974
1703	Reader, T. E.		
		Carrie Reader	22 Apr. 1932
5204	Real, Henry Francis		
		Santos F. Real	18 Oct. 1963
79259a	Reaves, Jill Brantley		
		William D. Reaves	21 Mar. 1980
4816	Redding, Pauline V.		
		O. K. Redding	31 Dec. 1959
83245a	Rediker, Rena Barbara		
		Dalton Rediker	30 Aug. 1984
2635	Reed, Adelaide Yarger		
		Alvin Reed	15 Mar. 1943
88247a	Reed, Myrtle Nell		
		Raymond Floyd Reed Jr.	18 Jan 1989

Case	Plaintiff	Defendant	Date
3339	Reed, Raley C.		
		Lynell Reed	20 Dec. 1948
4537	Reed, William D.		
		Maud C. Reed	21 Nov. 1957
2927	Reeder, Ella		
		Edward Reeder	25 Feb. 1946
3713	Reeh, Faye Vida		
		Raymond Chester Reeh	25 Sept. 1951
8299a	Reese, Callise Monet Allom		
		Douglas James Reese	15 Oct. 1982
6100	Reeves, Juanita M.		
		Royce E. Reeves	16 Oct. 1968
3190	Reeves, Wirt H.		
		Mildred F. Reeves	2 Feb. 1948
1874	Regenbreth, Lena		
		William Regenbreth	9 Oct. 1934
2739	Rehberger, Ferdinand		
		Frieda Rehberger	6 Sept. 1944
5656	Reichenau, Jerry Howard		
		Dorothy Fay Reichenau	7 July 1966
5530	Reichenser, Carol Jean		
		Marvin L. Reichenser	20 Nov. 1965
1739	Remschel, Claribel Dewees		
		Robert H. Remschel	20 Oct. 1932
88276a	Rendon, Callie Ann		
		Robert Rendon	31 May 1990
6495	Renfro, Cleo B.		
		Lowell E. Renfro	15 Sept. 1971
82189a	Resnick, Nancy Jane		
		Theodore Warren Resnick	3 Dec. 1982
1845	Reves, Marjorie		
		Floyd Reves	19 Apr. 1934
5944	Rexer, Bonnie W.		
		Joel P. Rexer	13 Oct. 1967
5663	Rexer, J. P.		
		Hazel G. Rexer	16 May 1966
5084	Reyes, Frances Bryant		
		John Reyes	25 Apr. 1962
7936a	Reyna, Sarah Ann		
		Jose Luis N. Reyna	21 June 1979
4633	Reynolds, Louise J.		
		Eugene Reynolds	24 July 1957
2204	Rhodes, Edward W.		
		Nellie Rhodes	20 Sept. 1938

Case	Plaintiff	Defendant	Date
5498	Rhodes, Elaine		
		Gene A. Rhodes	10 Dec. 1965
2989	Rhodes, George E. F.		
		Emma C. Rhodes	20 June 1946
4360	Rhodes, Henrietta Sybil		
		Raymond Lee Rhodes	7 Aug. 1956
6130	Rice, Billie Jean		
		Furmon C. Rice	18 Oct. 1968
85231a	Rice, Pauline Lopez		
		Victor Manuel Rice Jr.	17 Oct. 1986
87296a	Richard, Sherry Lynn		
		Buddie Richards	22 Aug. 1988
85216a	Richards, Sheryl L.		
		Mark H. Richards	27 Nov. 1985
5600	Richardson, Daisy M.		
		Conrad C. Richardson	9 Dec. 1965
8493a	Richardson, Kenny		
		Frieda Louise Richardson	
			12 July 1984
81138a	Rico, Antonio Jr.		
		Debra Sue Rico	13 Nov. 1981
2847	Ridley, Annie L.		
		Gilbert S. Ridley	4 Sept. 1945
3260	Ridenour, Isabel Cade		
		William Ridenour	14 June 1948
3666	Ridenour, Isabell		
		William Ridenour	18 June 1951
2302	Rieder, George E.		
		Wilhelmina Rieder	7 Oct. 1939
84233a	Riggsley, Lillian Dorothy		
		Norman C. Riggsley	3 Sept. 1985
6825	Riojas, Conception B.		
		Antonio Riojas	18 Jan. 1978
8119a	Rios, Ernestina M.		
		Joe Rios	19 June 1981
6855	Rios, Marie Evele		
		Isaac Ojeda Rios	18 Aug. 1977
87175a	Rios, Rosalie Morales		
		Javier C. Rios	16 Nov. 1987
5088	Ritchie, Sara		
		James C. Ritchie	7 June 1962
7937a	Rivera, Carolyn Sue		
		Gilbert Anthony Rivera	21 June 1979

Case	Plaintiff	Defendant	Date
83199a	Rivera, Gertrude Rosales		
		Orlando Rivera	23 Nov. 1983
5162	Roach, Mary M.		
		Charles R. Roach	18 Dec. 1962
2369	Roach, Vivian		
		David H. Roach	11 Mar. 1940
5358	Robbins, Mary Catherine		
		Herman Robbins	31 Aug. 1964
2351	Roberts, Edith		
		Henry Roberts	20 Sept. 1939
3401	Roberts, Elizabeth B.		
		Frank A. Roberts	22 June 1949
3023	Roberts, Henrietta		
		Curtis W. Roberts	3 Sept, 1946
1733	Roberts, Jessie		
		W. D. Roberts	22 Oct. 1932
2419	Roberts, Melassia Jane		
		Alexander C. Roberts	17 Sept. 1940
3739	Roberts, Pauline		
		Lonnie B. Roberts	7 Dec. 1951
4772	Roberts, Pauline		
		Lonnie B. Rogers	23 Sept. 1959
1906	Roberts, W. D.		
		Neola Roberts	29 Apr. 1935
4972	Robertson, Betty Louise		
		Adge Robertson Jr.	23 May 1961
4340	Robertson, Melissa Jane		
		Robt. L. Robertson	17 Dec. 1956
84186a	Robertson, Wanda		
		Elvis Robertson	23 May 1985
6048	Robinson, Lou Ellen		
		Robert Eugene Robinson	18 Oct. 1968
1824	Robinson, Minerva Holland		
		I. L. Robinson	16 Apr. 1934
2827	Rochell, Bernice		
		Lonnie Rochell	16 July 1945
5233	Rode, Charles H.		
		Evelyn Rode	21 Aug. 1963
5004a	Rodgers, Joe G.		
		Charlotte R. Rodgers	30 Oct. 1961
82234a	Rodgers, Loretta F.		
		Steven W. Rodgers	6 Jan. 1983
1773	Rodrigues, Ignacio		
		Luisa H.	17 Apr. 1933

Case	Plaintiff	Defendant	Date
80195a	Rodriguez, Alex M.		
		Idalene B. G. Rodriguez	
			23 Jan. 1981
3015	Rodriguez, Amalia		
		Blas L. Rodriguez	29 Oct. 1946
4858	Rodriguez, Emmett		
		Elinor Mae Stockton Rodriguez	
			9 June 1961
84381a	Rodriguez, Evangeline		
		Raymond Rodriguez	8 Feb. 1985
87275a	Rodriguez, Florentino Jr.		
		Vartha Rodriguez	20 Jan. 1988
3472	Rodriguez, Jesse		
		Myrtle Rodriguez	6 Feb. 1950
85122a	Rodriguez, Jose R.		
		Mary Esther G. Rodriguez	
			3 Sept. 1986
1955	Rodriguez, Lee A.		
		Alejandra Rodriguez	23 Oct. 1935
86113a	Rodriguez, Oralie Leal		
		Remigeo Rodriguez	30 June 1987
79266a	Rodriguez, Rebecca S.		
		Juan Jose Rodriguez	17 Jan. 1980
7960a	Rodriguez, Remijio		
		Petra R. Rodriguez	2 Aug. 1979
2106	Roe, Bertha		
		Nolan Roe	30 June 1937
4513	Roe, Frances Doyle		
		J. Claude Roe	7 Nov. 1957
2836	Roe, Veronah A.		
		James C. Roe	16 July 1945
4878	Rogers, Betty Lou		
		Donald Earl Rogers	28 July 1960
4170	Rogers, Ina Dale		
		Ward E. Rogers	9 Feb. 1955
4747	Rogers, J. H.		
		Ida Moore Rogers	6 July 1959
2789	Rogers, Julia		
		Proctor W. Rogers	8 June 1945
3410	Rogers, Lillie Rose		
		W. E. Rogers	18 July 1949
82172a	Rogers, Mark A.		
		Sylvia Ann Rogers	19 Nov. 1982

Case	Plaintiff	Defendant	Date
1649	Rogers, R. E.		
		Carrie Mae Rogers	6 Oct. 1931
3351a	Rogers, Stephanie W.		
		George W. Rogers	31 May 1983
3778	Rogers, Tressie		
		Robert Eli Rogers	27 Mar. 1952
3825	Rogers, W. E.		
		Cora Rogers	1 Aug. 1952
3972	Rogers, W. E.		
		Minnie Margaret Rogers	13 July 1953
8476a	Rogers, William Dudley		
		Paula Rogers	8 June 1984
2034.5	Rolph, Lula		
		Mennis Rolph	23 Oct. 1936
6271	Romero, Bobbie Ann Trigg		
		Louis Romero, Jr.	11 Dec. 1969
2654	Romero, Louis		
		Marie Torres Ramero	28 May 1943
88249a	Rosales, Diana Collazo		
		Roberto Alcada Rosales	13 Jan. 1989
2935	Rosales, Emiliano H.		
		Iginia Rosales	2 Feb. 1948
84223a	Rosales, Isidro A.		
		Beth L. Rosales	12 Oct. 1984
84293a	Rosales, Maria B.		
		Rudolph Rosales	31 July 1985
78144a	Rosales, Rachel Moreno		
		Richard Ricardo Rosales	31 May 1979
5536	Rosas, Gloria		
		Andrew Gilbert Rosas	30 Aug. 1965
3387	Rose, Betty Jane		
		Warren C. Rose	6 Sept. 1949
2183	Rose, Charlie		
		Nora May Rose	28 Mar. 1938
1700	Rose, Hattie Lundy		
		J. D. Rose	11 Apr. 1932
5273	Rosenbush, Shirley Faye		
		Melvin Rosenbush	20 Nov. 1963
86175a	Ross, Margaret		
		William Ross	19 Sept. 1986
2063	Rotge, Ora Mae		
		John Rotge	10 Oct. 1936
1740	Rotge, Ora Lee		
		John Rotge	22 Oct. 1932

Case	Plaintiff	Defendant	Date
1655	Rotge, Stella		
		Raymond Rotge	9 Oct. 1931
6165	Rotge, Vera		
		Robert Thos. Rotge	13 Jan. 1969
83174a	Rousley, Vern A.		
		Eleanor A. Rousley	8 Mar. 1984
7872a	Rowell, Zalah Mae		
		Joseph Cecil Rowell	1 Dec. 1978
8140a	Ruddy, John F.		
		Deanna M. Ruddy	29 June 1981
8395a	Rudolph, Marvin		
		Peggy S. Rudolph	24 Oct. 1983
2098	Ruff, Florence		
		George Ruff Jr.	30 Mar. 1937
5276	Ruiz, Paula		
		Pedro Ruiz	20 Nov. 1963
84172a	Rushing, Laura Ann		
		James Albert Rushing	18 Mar. 1985
6390	Russell, Bessie I.		
		Sherman A. Russell	28 May 1970
4303	Russell, Mary Louise		
		Wesley Edward Russell	19 Apr. 1956
5086	Rust, Glenda Lynn Merrett		
		Milton Rust	21 May 1962
80129a	Ruth, Ruth Elaine		
		Johnny Burns Ruth	30 July 1980
3712	Rutherford, Zula Cleo		
		Wm. L. Rutherford	23 Oct. 1951
4727	Rutledge, Laramae C.		
		Elias Rutledge	7 May 1959

S

Case	Plaintiff	Defendant	Date
1719	Saffarrens, Wanda		
		T. J. Saffarrens	5 Oct. 1932
8358a	Salentine, Judith Vivian		
		James Gordon Salentine	23 Aug, 1983
2325	Saludis, Adile S.		
		Wm. John Saludis	15 June 1939
87110a	Samford, Pamela Fay		
		Brookie Dale Samford	28 Sept, 1987
2358	Sample, E. E.		
		Ruth Sample	22 Sept. 1939

Case	Plaintiff	Defendant	Date
3915	Sanchez, Antonia Reyna		
		Raymond S. Sanchez	19 Sept. 1953
3110	Sanchez, Ben		
		Cruz Sanchez	18 Apr. 1947
7817a	Sanchez, Dellia Arreola Reyes		
		Reynaldo Flores Reyes	30 Aug. 1978
83193a	Sanchez, Elva Irene		
		Isidro Mejia Sanchez	27 Dec, 1984
2532	Sanchez, Francesco		
		Florine Sanchez	18 Mar. 1942
3658	Sanchez, Lillie		
		Ben Sanchez	18 Sept. 1951
2981	Sandefer, Sybil		
		Conway Sandefer	22 July 1946
5484	Sanders, John		
		Eva M. Sanders	20 May 1965
3291	Sandufer, Margaret		
		G. E. Sandufer	8 Sept. 1948
84302a	Sandoval, Esmeralda G.		
		Louis C. Sandoval	6 Mar. 1985
2902	Sandoval, Natalia		
		Manuel Sandoval	4 Mar. 1946
1956	Saner, R. C.		
		Bulah Saner	24 Oct. 1935
84168a	Sanski, Nancy Gail		
		Albin Joseph Sanski	16 Aaug. 1984
6296	Sansom, Don Wesley		
		Harriet M. Sansom	1 Oct. 1969
4120	Santos, Jose J.		
		Anita Santos	17 Sept. 1954
2652	Sarabia, Margaret		
		Lewis Sarabia	9 Sept. 1944
4802	Sarlls, Beatrice		
		Laurence K. Sarlls	14 Feb. 1960
8191a	Sauer, Keith Freeman		
		Irene Lumbreras Sauer	25 Feb. 1982
8213a	Sauer, Keith Freeman		
		Linda Sue James Sauer	22 Oct. 1982
8417a	Saunders, Alan W. Jr.		
		Connie Taylor Goodwin Saunders	
			24 May 1984
8314a	Saunior, Karen J.		
		Clyde E. Saunior	25 May 1983

Case	Plaintiff	Defendant	Date
8085a	Savage, Sandra Brainard		
		Lawrence R. Savage	27 June 1980
269	Sawyer, Sarah Jane		
		E. L. Sawyer	10 May 1889
3249	Scantling, Ruby L.		
		Homer B. Scantling	14 June 1948
1807	Scharck, Alma		
		Earnest Scharck	16 Oct. 1935
88206a	Schattel, Chris		
		Robert Anthony Schattel	20 Oct. 1989
88112a	Scheineman, Michael A.		
		Pamela K. Scheineman	19 Aug. 1988
7876a	Schellhase, Mary Zmergliker		
		Roland H. Schellhase	31 July 1979
2094	Scherrer, Louis		
		Lucy J Scherrer	31 Mar. 1937
3714	Schiller, Ida		
		Robert Schiller	8 Nov. 1951
5775	Schilling, Patsy Marie		
		Albert Schilling Jr.	13 Dec. 1966
4842	Schirch, Harry		
		Eunice J. Schirch	10 May 1961
8435a	Schlieter, Edward M.		
		Theda M. Schlieter	3 July 1985
6336	Schlinke, James C.		
		Judith Anne Schlinke	13 Mar. 1970
6186	Schlotzhauer, Richard M.		
		Virginia Louise Schlotzhauer	
			13 Mar. 1969
4861	Schlueter, Henry		
		Leona Schlueter	7 June 1960
84257a	Schlunegger, Ueli		
		Deborah Georgia Schluenegger	
			9 Nov. 1984
5546	Schmerber, Harold		
		Dorothy Louise Schmerber	
			27 Sept. 1965
7931a	Schmid, Debra Ann		
		Ronald Carson Schmid	10 May 1979
84167a	Schmidt, Arthur V.		
		Barbara Lee Schmidt	16 Aug. 1984
5010a	Schmidt, Helen Marie		
		Laurence Schmidt	12 Mar. 1962

Case	Plaintiff	Defendant	Date
5595	Schmidt, John		
		Betty Lou Schmidt	1 Apr. 1966
2610	Schmidtke, Fred		
		Annabell Schmidtke	1 Oct. 1942
6113	Schmidtke, Pauline Simonds		
		Robert Earl Schmidtke	9 Apr. 1970
2611	Schmidtke, R. E.		
		Ola Davoll Schmidtke	7 Oct. 1942
5664	Schneer, Anne		
		J. Y. Schneer	16 May 1966
79126a	Schneider, Delores F.		
		Eugene H. Schneider	13 Sept. 1979
1618	Schneider, Ella		
		Paul Schneider	23 Apr. 1931
5378	Schoenewolf, Irene Shulz		
		Harold F. Schoenewolf	4 Aug. 1964
5652	Schoenwolf, Irene		
		Harold Schoenwolf	1 Apr. 1966
5071	Schoenewolf, Minna		
		H. F. Schoenewolf	25 Apr. 1962
88131a	Schoolcraft, Charles Leslie		
		Bobbie T. Schoolcraft	24 Aug. 1988
4859	Schooler, Cora Bell		
		Bennie Lloyd Schooler	8 Jan. 1963
4160	Schreiber, Weldon Ervin		
		Willie Ruth Schreiber	14 Dec. 1954
8456a	Schreiner, Charles III		
		Lynore Murray Schreiner	15 May 1985
3456	Schreiner, Evaline F.		
		L. A. Schreiner	21 Oct. 1949
3208	Schrimscher, Mary Jo		
		W. A. Schrimscher	2 Feb. 1948
3907	Schuetze, Alma Bettie		
		Paul Schuetze	12 Feb. 1953
4845	Schuh, Irene		
		Frederich Schuh	1 Apr. 1961
2876	Schuh, John A.		
		Margaret Schuh	25 Feb. 1946
1785	Schult, Elsie		
		Werner Schult	12 July 1933
4221	Schumacher, Anita		
		Houston Schumacher	20 Feb. 1956
2863	Schuyler, Herberta		
		Clifford Schuyler	13 Nov. 1945

Case	Plaintiff	Defendant	Date
2377	Schwartz, Belle C.		
		Hy (?Henry) Schwartz	6 Mar. 1940
2837	Schwarz, Gordon H.		
		Elinor R. Schwarz	16 July 1945
82214a	Schwethelm, Lou Ann		
		W. C. Schwethelm	7 Dec. 1984
6152	Scoggins, Norris C. Jr.		
		Carol Lee Baker Low Scoggins	
			19 Dec. 1968
3930	Scoggins, Vivian B.		
		Norris Carroll Scoggins	13 Apr. 1953
4718	Scott, Bernice Opal		
		Wilber Guy Scott	31 Mar. 1959
3929	Scott, Leona		
		C. S. Scott	13 Apr. 1953
85182a	Scott, Leslie Dale Jr.		
		Heide Boerner Scott	24 Mar. 1986
82273a	Scott, Margaret		
		Robbie Harold Scott	18 Aug. 1983
8517a	Scott, Patricia Anne		
		Kingsbury Scott	1 July 1985
5903	Scott, Sharyn B.		
		Harrison L. Scott	3 Jan 1968
5945	Searcy, Linda Lou		
		Ronald Chas. Searcy	3 Oct. 1967
5280	Seifert, Enola P.		
		Jack M. Seifert	16 Dec. 1963
8357a	Seiva, Lynn Carol		
		Partick Paul Seiva	22 Aug. 1983
3099	Seltz, Doris		
		Jas. R. Seltz	15 Apr. 1947
5019	Sesson, Sandra		
		Harold C. Sesson	21 Aug. 1961
4591	Seward, Amy Merritt		
		Clarence Roscoe Seward	31 Mae. 1958
2631	Sewell, Betty		
		Epps H. Sewell	9 Mar. 1943
7998a	Sewell, Rosala Fay		
		Edward Anthony Sewell	2 Aug. 1979
4402	Seydler, Agnes		
		Erwin Herman Seydler	5 Jan. 1959
4494	Shaffer, Hilda		
		W. C. Shaffer	7 July 1959

Case	Plaintiff	Defendant	Date
82146a	Shannon, Larry L.		
		Dorothy J. Shannon	19 Nov. 1982
3927	Shannon, Vivian		
		Theodore Perry Shannon	
			22 Apr. 1953
83356a	Sharp, Joyce Marie		
		Thos. Ray Sharp	6 Mar. 1985
81187a	Sharp, Linda Sue		
		Thomas R. Sharp	13 Nov. 1981
3457	Sharp, Mary		
		Edwin King Sharp	12 Dec. 1949
3587	Sharp, Mary		
		Gerald A. Sharp	28 Nov. 1950
5528	Sharp, Shirley B.		
		Grady R. Sharp	30 July 1965
8436a	Sharp, Thomas R.		
		Linda S. Sharp	6 Apr. 1984
3209	Sharpe, Frances L. A. W.		
		Harry A. Sharpe	15 Dec. 1949
1985	Shelbourne, Mrs. A. L.		
		A. L. Shelbourne	31 Mar. 1936
2961	Shepard, Gladys		
		Burton Shepard	24 Apr. 1946
85324a	Shepard, Ruby Ann		
		Vernon Wayne Shepard	6 Mar. 1986
2742	Sheppard, J. L.		
		Mary Joe Sheppard	19 Dec. 1944
6726	Sheriff, LaDonna Ann		
		Randy Lewis Sheriff	5 Dec. 1975
6019	Sherman, Arlice		
		Henry Sherman	8 July 1968
80271a	Sherman, Keith Alan		
		Barbara Elaine Sherman	15 May 1981
4863	Sherman, Tommy Ruth		
		Marvin Sherman	1 Apr. 1961
86237a	Shields, Wanda Louise		
		Thos. Earl Shields	20 June 1988
5409	Shiflet, Pauline Roberts		
		Wm. H. Shiflet	19 Dec. 1964
86318a	Shifner, Lucretia		
		Jimmy Dale Shifner	4 Mar. 1987
5129	Shimp, Betty Sue		
		Wayne L. Shimp	10 June 1963

Case	Plaintiff	Defendant	Date
1596	Shirley, Mary Ida		
		Clifford Shirley	8 Apr. 1931
5451	Shirch, Anna Lou		
		Harry Shirch	12 Jan. 1965
80282a	Shoemake, Linda Susan		
		Timothy Dale Shoemake	20 Feb. 1981
6811	Shook, Sammie A.		
		Melvin C. Shook Jr.	29 Mar. 1977
4327	Short, Everett Donald		
		Marjorie Alline Short	11 June 1956
6220	Short, Janet Kay		
		Larry Don Short	16 May 1969
3901	Short, Marvin Clyde		
		Joyce Elaine Short	9 Feb. 1953
5095	Shubert, Irval		
		Grace Shubert	4 June 1962
79125a	Shubert, Josephine Fritz		
		Raymond Shubert	21 Sept. 1979
1841	Shumaker, Effie		
		George Shumaker	29 Mar. 1934
86306a	Shurtleff, Barbara Emile		
		James Orin Shurtleff	11 Feb. 1987
3403	Sidello, Mary		
		Andres Sidello	18 July 1949
4785	Sieker, Isle Mae		
		Robert Edward Sieker	14 Feb. 1959
4660	Sifford, Howard A.		
		Ola Mae Sifford	8 Dec. 1958
83224a	Sifford, Leona Amerentha		
		Russell Green Sifford	17 Feb. 1984
8080a	Sifford, Russell Green		
		Leona Amarithia Sifford	16 Jan. 1981
5154	Sigala, Nancy		
		Oscar C. Sigala	22 July 1963
2432	Silanis, Juanita V.		
		Ramon Silanis	29 Nov. 1940
81215a	Sill, Brenda J.		
		Larry C. Green Sill	30 July 1983
88272a	Silvs, Elida Huerto		
		Jesus M. Silva	15 Feb. 1989
3749	Silvas, Concha		
		Paul Silvas	11 Feb. 1952
2058	Silvas, Juan		
		Josephine Silvas	9 Oct. 1936

Case	Plaintiff	Defendant	Date
80221a	Simcoe, Robin L.		
		Gerald T. Simcoe	16 Jan. 1981
6030	Simmons, Darlene M.		
		Eugene E. Simmons	5 Aug. 1968
3096	Simmons, Joe B.		
		Billie D. Simmons	14 Apr. 1949
3601	Simmons, Lorraine		
		Ernest W. Simmons	19 Dec. 1950
4091	Simmons, Myrtle W.		
		Benj. F. Simmons	27 July 1954
4345	Simmons, Nellie Ault		
		Edwin Wm. Simmons	10 July 1956
88193a	Simmons, Randy S.		
		Katherine M. Simmons	11 Jan. 1989
85166a	Simmons, Roger Dale		
		Dana Inselman Simmons	6 July 1987
8692a	Simons, Deborah S.		
		Allen D. Simons	11 June 1986
8479a	Simpson, David B.		
		Karen Denise Simpson	24 May 1984
2209	Simpson, Gordon D.		
		Mamie Simpson	7 Oct. 1938
6944	Simpson, Wanda Arlene Taylor		
		Melvin Lester Simpson	16 Mar. 1978
3777	Sims, Willie		
		Lucille Sims	24 Mar. 1952
1673	Singletary, Iva		
		Joe Singletary	24 Oct. 1931
1778	Singleton, Loucile		
		Floyd E. Singleton	15 Apr. 1933
8570a	Sissney, Gayle Elaine Tuttle		
		David Glenn Sissney	20 Dec. 1985
4469	Sitter, Elton		
		Marie Sitter	12 Aug. 1957
1730	Skidmore, Effie		
		Carl Skidmore	13 Oct. 1932
5662	Skiles, E. M.		
		Carrie Skiles	7 June 1966
82280a	Skillern, Frances Areligh		
		Henry Rockwell Skillern	25 Mar. 1983
83146a	Skinner, Jeri Ann		
		Billy Rae Skinner	14 Oct. 1983
2859	Skipworth, O. N.		
		Willie Mae Skipworth	14 Sept. 1945

Case	Plaintiff	Defendant	Date
8210a	Sklar, David Sylvester		
		Yvonne Marie Sklar	26 May 1982
88105a	Skurupey, Lisa		
		Michael Dean Skurupey	4 Aug. 1988
2951	Slaven, Madeline		
		Connie Slaven	22 Apr. 1946
8472a	Sloan, Stephen Davis		
		Edna Malliere Sloan	30 Aug. 1984
2051	Slusher, Ruby		
		Walter Slusher	8 Oct. 1936
5059	Smith, Bernard F.		
		Dorisa Helene Smith	5 Jan. 1962
2609	Smith, Bob		
		Lilly Mae Smith	28 Sept. 1942
4831	Smith, C. J. Jr.		
		Darlene Emma Kordzik Wells Smith	27 Feb. 1961
4981	Smith, Della		
		Seth A. Smith	10 May 1961
89270a	Smith, Donald W.		
		Isabel V. Smith	20 Feb. 1981
5413	Smith, Earlene		
		Seth A. Smith	17 Nov. 1964
85107a	Smith, Jo Anne Liese		
		Mike C. Smith	23 Dec. 1986
8320a	Smith, Johnye Marie		
		Billy Frank Smith	24 Mar. 1983
85282a	Smith, Kevin S.		
		Carol R. Smith	3 Jan. 1986
5634	Smith, Leona B.		
		Arvin Smith	16 Mar. 1966
2607	Smith, Lilly Mae		
		Bob Smith	25 Sept. 1942
4286	Smith, Lois Marie		
		Geo. Daniel Smith	25 Jan. 1956
5384	Smith, Mary Lee		
		Bernard F. Smith	2 Sept. 1964
4681	Smith, Maxine		
		Graydon Smith	8 Dec. 1958
82213a	Smith, Patricia Ann		
		Lannie Wayne Smith	6 Jan. 1982
87190a	Smithson, Arel		
		Benjamin Forest Smithson	19 Nov. 1987

Case	Plaintiff	Defendant	Date
88172a	Smyers, Terry S.		
		Scott M. Smyers	25 Jan. 1989
3528	Smyre, Mary		
		Charles O. Smyre	19 May 1950
2027	Snelgrove, George F.		
		Willie Mae Snelgrove	12 Apr. 1937
85278a	Snider, Maria Sherman		
		Dwight Fitzgerald Snider	13 May 1986
5567	Snowdon, Lena B.		
		Willie J. Snowdon	6 Nov. 1965
79284a	Snyder, Peggy Weyrich		
		Chas. Albert Snyder	28 Mar. 1980
1864	Solomon, Jessie J.		
		Frances Solomon	10 Oct. 1934
80183a	Solomon, Saluna Lou		
		James Richard Solomon	2 Feb. 1981
3829	Solono, Michael		
		Jane Solono	15 Dec. 1952
4164	Somers, Beulah Mae		
		William L. Somers	12 Aug. 1955
4725	Somers, Earl		
		Omagene Somers	26 Mar. 1959
88198a	Sorell, Ed Martin		
		Sandra Sue Schwethelm Sorell	28 Apt. 1989
3548	Sorsby, Ann J.		
		Cecil Sorsby	25 Apr. 1951
2967	Soto, Bertha		
		Simon Soto	30 May 1946
83234a	Southammeroy, Seng		
		Harry Southammeroy	27 Jan 1984
7829a	Spaeth, Leon P.		
		Ruth Brown Spaeth	31 Aug. 1978
5201	Spangler, Lillian E.		
		Virgil V. Spangler	13 May 1963
3962	Sparks, H. Cecil		
		Frances Jean Sparks	13 July 1953
83169a	Sparks, Laura Lee		
		James Garvis Sparks	27 Jan. 1984
3968	Sparrow, Leda		
		Newport Sparrow	13 July 1953
8489a	Spearman, Laura Lee		
		James Vinyard Spearman	21 June 1964

Case	Plaintiff	Defendant	Date
3533	Spears, Charlotte T.		
		Richard K. Spears Jr.	26 Sept. 1950
3208	Spellman, Eva Mae		
		Willis Spellman	6 Nov. 1947
5934	Spencer, Sandra G.		
		Joe O. Spencer	8 Sept. 1967
84243a	Spencer, Shirley Ann		
		Stephen Dale Spencer	9 Nov. 1984
3121	Spenrath, Dan Jr.		
		Ruth Spenrath	9 June 1947
8248a	Spenrath, Dona Jean		
		Larry Arthur Spenrath	28 May 1982
6058	Spenrath, Madelene		
		Ralph Walter Spenrath	30 July 1968
3298	Spiser, Maurine		
		Edgar C. Spiser	28 Oct. 1948
3487	Spraggens, Arvin		
		Cornelia O. Spraggens	6 Feb. 1950
81129a	Spratt, Arra Leaine		
		Kenneth Thayer Spratt	20 Nov. 1981
3018	Spurgeon, Lorraine		
		Wayne Spurgeon	3 Sept. 1946
6034	Stacy, Janis M.		
		George Leon Stacy	23 May 1968
5361	Stacy, Shirley Ruth		
		George Leon Stacy	31 Aug. 1964
6413	Staggs, Diane J.		
		Steven W. Staggs	10 June 1970
4290	Stamps, Etta Mae		
		Eddie Lee Stamps	11 June 1956
2634	Stancill, Edgar A.		
		Bertha Stancill	2 Apr. 1943
2692	Stansbury, Beulah		
		Landry Stansbury	6 Dec. 1943
2966	Stapleton, Joyce E.		
		William Z. Stapleton	5 June 1946
4403	Stapleton, Margaret		
		Wm. Z. Stapleton	31 Mar. 1957
1727	Starkey, Rachael Smith		
		Horace J. Starkey	8 Oct. 1932
2472	Starkey, Sarah K.		
		G. Rankin Starkey	11 Mar. 1941
5045	Staudt, Anne Olson		
		Sid Staudt	30 Oct. 1961

Case	Plaintiff	Defendant	Date
5980	Staudt, Delores Lorraine		
		William Emil Staudt	20 Dec. 1967
3663	Steele, Anita R.		
		Bristol A. Steele	18 Sept. 1953
4993	Steelman, Ruth Bussey		
		Fred E. Smith	8 June 1961
3027	Steen, Marie		
		Leonard Steen	2 Jan. 1947
8255a	Steffey, Jon G.		
		Janet A. Steffey	28 May 1982
2602	Stegall, Jessie M.		
		John H. Stegall	8 Mar. 1943
3686	Stehling, Alois		
		Juneda E. Stehling	13 Sept. 1951
79178a	Stehling, Anton R.		
		Anna Laverne Stehling	1 July 1980
6370	Steiner, William J.		
		Nancy Elaine Pollard Steiner	28 Jan. 1970
8153a	Stell, Joseph Harry Jr.		
		Margaret Kathryn Stell	7 May 1981
7994a	Stephens, A. Kay		
		Hughey B. Stephens	1 Nov. 1979
3884	Stephens, Amy Merritt		
		Jack Stephens	15 Dec. 1952
6541	Stephens, Elton		
		Donna Ray Stephens	25 Jan. 1972
5164	Stephens, Gloria Jeanette		
		John T. Stephens	8 Jan. 1963
1894	Stephens, Jack		
		Annie Stephens	26 Oct. 1934
2626	Stephens, Jack		
		Connie Stephens	2 Apr. 1943
5671	Stephens, John Allen		
		Sharon Stephens	21 May 1966
6890	Stephens, Rita Carol		
		Donald M. Stephens Jr.	19 Nov. 1979
79105a	Stephens, Rita Charlene		
		Jerry B. Stephens	4 Oct. 1979
5269	Stephens, Sharon Nicole		
		John Allen Stephens	18 Oct. 1963
2668	Stephens, Vera		
		Jack Stephens	18 May 1944

Case	Plaintiff	Defendant	Date
5840	Stephenson, Mary Louise		
		C. W. Stepehnson	22 Mar. 1967
6463	Stevens, Peggy A.		
		Earl D. Stevens	6 Nov. 1970
6384	Stevens, Maurice Evelyn		
		James Edell Stevens	1 May 1970
3055	Stevens, Nina		
		Leonard M. Stevens	2 Jan. 1947
2443	Stevens, Roberta F.		
		Jas. Edell Stevens	17 Sept. 1940
4154	Stevens, Roy T.		
		Rose Marie Stevens	6 Dec. 1954
3753	Stevens, Thelma Jean		
		Wm. Douglas Stvens	14 Feb. 1952
5102	Stevenson, Roger		
		Nell Stevenson	21 May 1962
2248	Stewart, Eloise		
		T. R. Stewart	7 Mar. 1939
5183	Stewart, Linda K.		
		James Edward Stewart	27 Mar. 1963
2415	Stewart, Linnie D.		
		J. D. Stewart	18 Aug. 1949
2756	Stieler, Ola		
		Eugene A. Stieler	19 Dec. 1944
5758	Stoepler, Mona Ruth		
		Herry Leslie Stoepler	2 Dec. 1966
6089	Stokes, Brown H.		
		Barbara Ann Stokes	20 Sept. 1968
81198a	Stokes, Dianna Jane		
		Billy Ray Stokes	4 Feb. 1982
5977	Stoltz, Careol M.		
		Robert L. Stoltz	20 Dec. 1967
4915	Stone, Jimmy Lee		
		William H. Stone	10 Jan. 1961
6414	Stone, John R.		
		Eloise B. Stone	18 May 1970
86314a	Stone, Mary Ella		
		Lindell Theo. Stone	8 Apr. 1987
4473	Stone, Mildred Inez		
		Anton Clark Stone	24 June 1957
2163	Stone, Roger		
		Pauline Stone	4 Oct. 1937
2581	Stone, Ura D.		
		Cecil J. Stone	16 Mar. 1942

Case	Plaintiff	Defendant	Date
2473	Stone, Ura D.		
		Cecil Jackson Stone	17 Mar. 1941
4525	Stone, William H.		
		Edna Marie Stone	25 Oct. 1957
8484a	Storms, Lrene Elaine		
		Chas. Lawton Storms	21 June 1984
4213	Stotts, Charlsie Fay		
		Chas. Bennett Stotts	12 Aug. 1955
82275a	Stotts, Muriel Brenda		
		Ronald Roy Stotts	25 May 1983
4567	Stotts, Vivian E.		
		Charles B. Stotts	28 Apr. 1958
5259	Stovall, Lois Rheams		
		Chas. Ross Stovall	16 Dec. 1963
85261a	Stovall, Wesley J.		
		Barbara E. Stovall	19 Dec. 1985
84209a	Strackbein, Barbara Noretta		
		Howard Dean Strackbein	12 Oct. 1984
81179a	Strackbein, Kathleen Ann		
		Gary Wayne Strackbein	26 Oct. 1981
2627	Strather, Lee		
		Mable Strather	16 Mar. 1943
4387	Strats, Hazel Grona		
		Frederick Chas. Strats	29 Oct. 1956
2343	Strauch, Esther		
		Scott G. Strauch	19 Sept. 1939
4957a	Strauss, Richla Kay		
		Homer Charles Strauss Jr.	
			21 Nov. 1979
5892	Strego, Laura Johnson		
		Fred Strego	29 June 1967
7975a	Strickland, Sandra K.		
		James E. Strickland	2 Aug. 1979
2862	Stricklin, Mary		
		George W. Stricklin	25 Feb. 1946
5478	Stringer, George Henry		
		Effie Edwards Stringer	1 June 1965
84272a	Strube, Harold Wayne		
		Vickie J. Strube	7 Mar. 1985
1895	Stueler, Ruby		
		Beno Stueler	26 Oct. 1934
2864	Sturdevant, Hazel		
		John R. Sturdevant	8 Oct. 1945

Case	Plaintiff	Defendant	Date
1599	Sublett, Neva Tarver		
		Virgil Sublett	31 Mar. 1931
85230a	Sullivan, Delbert		
		Loleta P. Sullivan	19 Aug. 1986
84325a	Sullivan, Jody		
		Marcus Scott Sullivan	24 Jan. 1985
81118a	Sullivan, Mary Eliz.		
		John Timothy Sullivan	4 Nov. 1981
2402	Sullivan, W. R.		
		Edna F. Sullivan	17 Sept. 1940
2076	Summers, Della		
		Ernest F. Summers	7 Apr. 1937
3823	Surber, Lucille		
		Louis Surber	12 Aug. 1952
4202	Sutherland, Ruth M.		
		Shelton Sutherland	12 Aug. 1955
1635	Suttles, Homer		
		Katherine Suttles	6 Oct. 1931
6210	Sutton, Lewis S.		
		Eugenia S. Sutton	8 May 1969
6059	Sutton, Ruth Blalock		
		Harry V. Sutton	20 Sept. 1968
5781	Sweatmen, Melvin R.		
		Mary Frances Sweatman	7 Mar. 1967
5965	Sweatt, Zona Hollcomb		
		Irvin Willis Sweatt	25 Oct. 1967
6281	Swim, Connie G.		
		Christine M. Swim	23 Mar. 1971
3934	Swing, L. Anna		
		R. P. Swing	22 Apr. 1952
8722a	Switzer, Chas. Edward		
		Terumi Matsuguma Switzer	21 Apr. 1987
6987	Switzer, Sandra Van Ostrand		
		Michael Allen Switzer	21 Feb. 1978
4367	Sykes, Ruth		
		Willie Sykes	14 Aug. 1956

T

Case	Plaintiff	Defendant	Date
2760	Talbert, Alberta		
		Arthur Talbert	18 Jan. 1945
8899a	Tales, Rex Leroy		
		Martha Velaquez Teles	3 Mar. 1988

Case	Plaintiff	Defendant	Date
3242	Tamplin, Margaret L.		
		Jack D. Tamplin	26 Apr. 1948
3580	Tant, Minnie Viola		
		Robert Lee Tant	25 Apr. 1951
3107	Tate, Christine		
		Edward W. Tate	26 Mar. 1947
4778	Taylor, Barbara A.		
		R. B. Taylor	14 Dec. 1959
4892	Taylor, Charles A.		
		Clara Geneva Taylor	18 Jan. 1961
7980a	Taylor, Eddie Ernest		
		Bonnie Taylor	29 May 1980
3019	Taylor, Ellen		
		V. H. Taylor	3 Sept. 1946
3388	Taylor, Elmo M.		
		Irma Lucille Taylor	19 May 1949
2359	Taylor, Eva R.		
		Marvin E. Taylor	26 Sept. 1939
1947	Taylor, F. E.		
		Edith Marie Taylor	16 Oct. 1935
3853	Taylor, Henry I.		
		Victoria V. Taylor	22 Apr. 1953
83230a	Taylor, Jacqueline Annette		
		Richard Wesley Taylor	4 Jan. 1984
2595	Taylor, Jas. W.		
		Nona M. Taylor	22 Sept. 1942
5756	Taylor, Jerry		
		Janice Morris Taylor	20 Feb. 1967
4056	Taylor, Jo Anne		
		Robert W. Taylor	14 May 1954
4752	Taylor, John P.		
		Dorothy H. Taylor	28 Aug. 1959
7839a	Taylor, Lazetta E.		
		William W, Taylor IV	20 Oct. 1978
4259	Taylor, Lorene		
		Lawrence L. Taylor	26 Nov. 1955
836a	Taylor, Marjorie Marie		
		Melvin/Milton Wayne Taylor	
			24 Mar. 1983
79102a	Taylor, Marjorie Mc Cracken		
		Melvin Wayne Taylor	5 Sept. 1979
4424	Taylor, Mary		
		Lawrence Taylor	3 June 1957

Case	Plaintiff	Defendant	Date
78141a	Taylor, Milton Eugene		
		An B. Taylor	6 June 1979
2908	Taylor, Nannie		
		Haskell Taylor	25 Feb. 1946
8818a	Taylor, Olivia Christine		
		Thos. Dewayne Taylor	20 Apr. 1988
3575	Taylor, Rudolph H.		
		Myrtle M. Taylor	14 Nov. 1950
7874a	Taylor, Sandra Kathryn		
		Tom J. Taylor	14 Feb. 1979
5741	Taylor, Violet		
		Sam H. Taylor	15 Nov. 1966
3038	Taylor, William A.		
		Lela Mae Taylor	25 Oct. 1946
5172	Teague, Leslie		
		Jennie Teague	7 Mar. 1963
61	Tegner, Fritz		
		Susan E. Tegner	31 May 1866
3035	Temple, Madeline		
		Thomas L. L. Temple	7 Nov. 1946
3661	Terry, Bessie		
		Marvin Terry	18 June 1951
5875	Terry, Hattie K.		
		Roy P. Terry	12 Feb. 1968
4723	Terry, Louella		
		Leslie Terry	7 May 1959
88269a	Terry, Lynn Taylor		
		Robert Allen Terry Sr.	1 Mar. 1989
827a	Terry, Patricia Lee Campbell		
		Richard Randall Terry	7 Apr. 1982
5149	Thacker, Bobbie Sue		
		Wayne D. Thacker	14 Dec. 1962
84276a	Thaler, Louis Randy Jr.		
		Dianne Lynn Thaler	15 Dec. 1984
4542	Theobald, Theresa		
		William Theobald Jr.	24 Mar. 1959
4625	Thomas, Dorothy Ellen		
		Walter Leslie Thomas	13 Oct. 1958
6242	Thomas, Franklin R.		
		Gloria Jean Thomas	3 Cot. 1969
1753	Thomas, James		
		Margaret H. Thomas	20 Apr. 1934
84323a	Thomas, Jerald Lewis		
		Julie Gaye Perle Thomas	8 Feb. 1985

Case	Plaintiff	Defendant	Date
5170	Thomas, Martha		
		Daniel Thomas	7 Jan. 1963
8829a	Thomas, Tanya R.		
		Nelton Thomas Jr.	20 Apr. 1988
4291	Thomas, Walter		
		Laureal Eddie M. Thomas	2 Mar. 1956
2559	Thompson, C. C.		
		Ida B. Thompson	9 Mar. 1942
5659	Thompson, Carolyn Sue Moore		
		Laurence Thompson	22 Apr. 1966
3193	Thompson, Jas. W.		
		Mary J. Thompson	4 Mar. 1948
8423a	Thompson, Jewell Blanche		
		Lloyd J. Thompson	26 Apr. 1984
3785	Thompson, Jimmie W.		
		Christine Thompson	25 Mar. 1952
2790	Thompson, Juanelle		
		Lee B. Thompson	5 Apr. 1945
85124a	Thompson, Kellie Lucille		
		Stephen Frank Thompson	28 Aug. 1985
1892	Thompson, Laura		
		Millard Thompson	16 Oct. 1934
5249	Thompson, Millie A.		
		Pete C. Thompson	1 Sept. 1964
8497a	Thompson, Patricia Annette		
		Roy Newton Thompson	8 June 1984
7969a	Thompson, Robert Ray		
		Ina Jean Thompson	28 Dec. 1979
85167a	Thorne, Ruth M.		
		Anthony Thorne	8 Nov. 1985
4809	Thorp, Susie Bell		
		Draydon J. Thorp	19 Dec. 1959
1831	Thurman, A. J. Jr.		
		Bessie Thurman	27 Mar. 1934
5359	Thurman, Dorothy M.		
		Foster A. Thurman	7 Dec. 1964
2767	Thurman, Jno. J.		
		Etta Ruth Thurman	19 Dec. 1944
5580	Tillson, Mable Mae		
		Wm. L. Tillson Jr.	20 Nov. 1965
845a	Tilton, Debra Lynne		
		Michael Douglas Tilton	24 May 1984
84256a	Tischler, Thomas Henry		
		Doris Lee Tischler	27 Dec. 1984

Case	Plaintiff	Defendant	Date
4248	Todham, H. A.		
		Eugenia A. Todham	9 Nov. 1955
1896	Toler, Cedric		
		Emma L. Toler	18 Oct. 1933
4614	Toler, Myrtle E.		
		Fred Toler	9 June 1958
88199a	Tolman, Hilda A.		
		Ernest Bernard Tolman	16 Jan. 1990
2180	Tompkins, Clifford E.		
		Verna M. Thompkins	9 Mar. 1938
2596	Tompkins, Nettie		
		F. D. Thompkins	7 Aug. 1942
8676a	Tomlinson, Judy Anne		
		Tommy Reid Tomlinson	29 May 1986
2555	Tonahill, Maxine		
		H. L. Tonahill	11 Apr. 1942
8147a	Tonnessen, Linda W.		
		Roger W. Tonnessen	4 Feb. 1982
4608	Tonnessen, Mabel		
		Richard William Tonnessen	
			5 June 1958
1828	Towns, Ettyline		
		Sylvester Towns	29 Mar. 1934
3069	Townsend, Charlene D.		
		Elbert W. Townsend	2 Jan. 1947
80175a	Townsend, James E.		
		Margaret S. Townsend	17 Oct. 1980
85274a	Townsend, Peter		
		Kate A. Townsend	19 Dec. 1985
80197a	Trainum, Martin H.		
		Pamela Fay Trainum	29 Oct. 1980
5702	Trapp, Howard		
		Mary Jo Trapp	28 Apr. 1967
2166	Traveland, Odin		
		Telva Traveland	26 Jan. 1938
84164a	Traweek, Jimmy Wade		
		Jarga Jo Traweek	28 Mar. 1985
4244	Treadwell, Doris F.		
		Kenneth Treadwell	24 Sept, 1955
8035a	Treadwell, Irby Kay		
		Johnny Ray Treadwell	1 May 1980
4595	Treadwell, Jo Ann		
		Wm. A. Treadwell	13 Oct. 1958

Case	Plaintiff	Defendant	Date
3478	Treiber, Ruth Lillie		
		Gottlieb Herman Treiber	12 Dec. 1949
86284a	Trempe, Chas. Wallace		
		Brenda Lee Schmidt Trempe	
			15 May 1987
1846	Trevino, Cruze		
		David Trevino	4 Apr. 1934
87297a	Trevino, Gabriel Q.		
		Angie L. Trevino	16 Mar. 1988
5589	Trevino, Jean		
		Arthur Trevino	20 Nov. 1965
2499	Trevino, Jesus		
		Isabel Trevino	17 Sept. 1941
4046	Trevino, Lupe		
		Frank Trevino	14 May 1954
3976	Trigo, Estella Garza		
		Antonio S. Trigo	2 Feb. 1954
8065a	Trost, Nancy Jane		
		Chas. Douglas Trost	30 July 1980
5523	Truelove, Myrtle Callahan		
		Melvin Truelove	6 Nov. 1965
8764a	Truesdall, Gerald Don		
		Paula Louis Truesdall	10 June 1987
4830	Truman, Minnie Belle		
		Henry Lewis Truman	19 Apr. 1960
4626	Truscott, Jinnie		
		Beatrice Truscott	13 Oct. 1958
8799a	Tuma, Jeannine Theresa		
		Kenneth Richard Tuma	8 Sept. 1987
5410	Turley, Larry D.		
		Rosa Darlene Turley	2 Nov. 1964
1695	Turmon, Annie E.		
		John F. Turmon	4 Apr. 1932
3746	Turner, Dorothy S.		
		Kenneth W. Turner	24 Mar. 1952
6170	Turner, Kenella M.		
		Leon R. Turner	14 Jan 1969
80202a	Turner, Larell Powell		
		Jeffery Owen Turner	27 Feb. 1981
6967	Turner, Linda Jane		
		Michael Wayne Turner	9 Jan 1978
1617	Turner, Louise		
		Charles Turner	21 Apr. 1931

Case	Plaintiff	Defendant	Date
2612	Turner, Pauline		
		Claude R. Turner	9 Nov. 1942
2658	Turner, T. W.		
		Ora Turner	8 Sept. 1943
3585	Tyler, Cleo		
		Leslie Tyler	28 Nov. 1950
5188	Tyner, Dorothy Lee		
		Harbin Tyner	15 July 1963

U

Case	Plaintiff	Defendant	Date
5575	Ulery, Fayebelle		
		Oliver L. Ulery	23 Aug. 1965
2488	Upton, Effie Dell		
		Louis Mc Corskey Upton	18 Mar. 1941
2807	Upton, Effie Dell		
		Louise Mc Croskey Upton	16 July 1945
6441	Urias, Sostenes Jr.		
		Lulabelle I. Urias	30 June 1970

V

Case	Plaintiff	Defendant	Date
2957	Valderas, Georgenna R.		
		Joe Valderas	5 June 1946
784a	Valdez, Beatrice		
		Joe Valdez	16 Mar. 1979
83238a	Valdez, Christine		
		Joe Valdez	12 July 1984
5838	Valdez, Emilio		
		Lillie Valdez	6 June 1967
5920	Valdez, Eva		
		Tony Valdez	18 Oct. 1968
2064	Valdez, Frances		
		Joe Valdez	10 Oct. 1936
8487a	Valenzuela, Marie Nieves		
		Antonio Valenzuela	11 July 1985
1767	Vallier, Jesus		
		V. J. Vallier	8 Oct. 1938
6887	Vanden, W. T.		
		Joyce Virginia Vanden	20 Oct. 1977
2931	Vandever, Ilra Bella		
		Paschel G. Vandever	22 Apr. 1946

Case	Plaintiff	Defendant	Date
8381a	Vandevort, Barbara	Chadwick Roddy Vandevort	7 Oct. 1983
2145	Van Drome, Louis J.	Louise M. Van Drome	14 Mar. 1938
4753	Van Gorder, Dorothy	Francis Clem Van Gorder	6 July 1959
80243a	Vankirk, Ilyne C.	Charles Leroy Vankirk	7 Apr. 1981
1993	Vann, Charles C.	Josephine Vann	31 Mar. 1936
5417	Vaquera, Irene S.	Pete Tovar Vaquera	17 Nov. 1964
3842	Varner, Newton D.	Stella Varner	12 Sept. 1953
2845	Vasser, Mary E.	Roy W. Vasser	14 Sept. 1945
8531a	Vaughn, Kimberly Ann	John Richard Vaughn	24 Apr. 1985
87189a	Vaughn, Shirley Ruth	Alton Seamore Vaughn	16 Dec. 1987
8797a	Vaughn, Susana Nichols	Timothy Vaughn	8 June 1988
1823	Villaneuva, Leandro	Margreta Villaneuva	31 Mar. 1934
6253	Villareal, Linda O.	Paul A. Villareal	30 July 1969
3142	Villarreal, Fostina	Roman R. Villarreal	18 July 1949
8552a	Villarreal, Oralia R.	Hilberto L. Villarreall	3 Sept. 1987
8334a	Vinas, Joseph Francis	Beverly Renee Vinas	23 June 1983
3094	Vincent, Jane	George Vincent	15 Apr. 1947
6260	Virdell, Eunice Arleen	Archie Rex Virdell	24 July 1969
6275	Vlasek, Donna	William E. Vlasek	1 Oct. 1969
6980	Vlasek, Doris Elaine	Frank David Vlasek	19 Jan. 1978
5586	Vogt, Harvey E.	Bobbie Dee Vogt	6 Nov. 1965

Case	Plaintiff	Defendant	Date
5635	Vogt, Harvey E.		
		Bobbie Dee Vogt	21 Sept. 1966
5821	Vollmer, Diane G.		
		Lindon D. Vollmer	13 June 1967
5414	Vollmer, Linden D.		
		Malinda Farrin Vollmer	16 Dec. 1964
85128a	Voulgaris, James Constantine		
		Sharla Kay Voulgaris	23 Oct. 1985

W

Case	Plaintiff	Defendant	Date
8442a	Wadiwalla, Frances		
		Alatef Wadiwalla	26 Apr. 1984
87282a	Wafford, David Joe		
		Marianne D. Wafford	7 Dec. 1988
85313a	Wagoner, Russell Dean		
		Carol Louise Wagoner	24 Mar. 1986
87165a	Wagner, Elizabeth Ann		
		J. D. Wagner	16 Feb. 1988
84175a	Wagner, Randall Eugene		
		Veronica Kay Wagner	16 Aug. 1984
80166a	Wagner, Sheila Ann Parish		
		Rickey Dean Wagner	19 June 1981
4057	Wahrmund, Stella Peiper		
		George Wahrmund	26 July 1954
3994	Waite, Thelam		
		Richard A. Waite	11 Sept. 1953
83135a	Walker, Alexander Stuart		
		Shirley Ann Walker	18 Sept. 1983
3963	Walkler, Arlilina		
		R. S. T. Waller	16 July 1953
4119	Walker, Elsie		
		Roy Walker	16 Sept. 1954
4193	Walker, Hershal O. Jr.		
		Blanch Walker	9 Apr. 1955
81242a	Walker, Howard Wayne		
		Madelynn Carroll Walker	25 Feb. 1983
2355	Walker, Ida Jasper		
		Willie Walker	19 Sept. 1939
4139	Walker, Polly Ware		
		Benj. A. Walker	6 Dec. 1954
1632	Walker, Ruby		
		Leonard Walker	6 Oct. 1931

Case	Plaintiff	Defendant	Date
1722	Wall, Lena		
	H. R. Wall		4 Oct. 1932
86292a	Wall, Randy I.		
	Norene Wall		16 Sept, 1987
1693	Wallace, J. H.		
	Ruby Wallace		4 Apr. 1932
3451	Wallace, Martha G.		
	Ross P. Wallace		13 Oct. 1949
8393a	Wallace, Ronald Douglas Sr.		
	Elma Ann Moss Wallace		23 June 1983
3278	Wallace, Ronnie		
	Johnnie Wallace		8 Sept. 1948
4664	Walters, Adam C.		
	Alice Walters		30 Oct. 1958
5559	Walters, Carolyn L.		
	Jerry L. Walters		6 Oct. 1965
4568	Walzer, Billie Charlene		
	Francis M. Walzer		23 Jan. 1958
6025	Walzer, Floyd		
	Frank Walzer		18 Oct. 1970
6114	Wampler, Verna B.		
	Albert N. Wampler		9 Sept. 1968
84288a	Wann, Nina Demaree Woodward		
	Lowell Eugene Wann		8 May 1985
8765a	Warden, Charles Wm.		
	Mary Lott Warden		3 June 1987
3353	Ware, Lincoln		
	Frances Ware		15 Oct. 1950
3479	Warlick, J. H.		
	Gertrude H. Warlick		27 Dec. 1949
3305	Warlick, John H.		
	Rose Warlick		25 Oct. 1948
2485	Warren, Ellis Edward		
	Susie Mae Warren		11 Mar. 1941
81165a	Warren, Joe A.		
	Wanda Gloria Warren		2 Oct. 1981
83190a	Warren, Lary D.		
	Sherry Jane Warren		23 Nov. 1983
4757	Warren, Violet		
	Harry Warren		14 Sept. 1959
7838a	Washburn, Raynell Dorothea		
	Billy Niel Washburn		10 Oct. 1978

Case	Plaintiff	Defendant	Date
2993	Washington, Ella		
		Johnnie Washington	22 July 1946
82119a	Waters, Wesley		
		Pamela M. Waters	5 Nov. 1982
85281a	Watson, Andrea J.		
		Ronald Keith Watson	3 Jan. 1986
3052	Watson, Johnnie T.		
		Virginia Watson	2 Jan. 1947
85188a	Watson, Larue		
		Hayward Watson	17 Apr. 1986
1691	Watson, Maud Ruth		
		Farris Joel Watson	29 Mar. 1932
87102a	Watson, Raymond J. Jr.		
		Brenda J. Watson	16 July 1987
8322a	Watson, William Robert		
		Dianne E. Watson	7 Apr. 1983
85143a	Wauhop Kathy		
		Donald E. Waurop	23 Jan. 1986
5440	Way, Wanda Nell		
		Kenneth Richard Way	26 Jan. 1965
79287a	Weatherby, Frances Jo		
		Dan A. Weatherby	5 May 1981
8457a	Weatherley, Dana Jr.		
		Frances Jo Weatherley	26 July 1984
2370	Weaver, Rose G.		
		Jack C. Weaver	4 Oct. 1939
843a	Weaver, Sylvia Elaine		
		Paige Vargas Weaver	6 Mar. 1985
3191	Webb, Ethel		
		Upton Webb	15 Dec. 1947
87223a	Webb, James Carroll		
		Laura Lee Webb	3 May 1989
2148	Webb, Lois		
		Fred A. Webb	28 Sept. 1937
2782	Webb, Upton		
		Ethel Webb	5 Apr. 1945
7824a	Webber, Amber Wood		
		James Lial Webber	21 Nov. 1978
3234	Weddle, Nell		
		James D. Weddle	27 Apr. 1948
7954a	Wedin, John H.		
		Georgia M. Wedin	3 July 1979
81160a	Wehmeyer, Patsy Ann		
		Karl L. Wehmeyer	22 Sept. 1981

Case	Plaintiff	Defendant	Date
3969	Wehrs, Thora Helen		
		Henry H. Wehrs	2 Nov. 1953
79100a	Weimer, James Russell		
		Sharon Lynette Wilton Weimer	19 Dec. 1979
6368	Weiner, Ethel Mae		
		Lloyd Laurence Weiner	4 Feb. 1970
5695	Weisner, Shirley Frances		
		James Albert Weisner	3 Apr. 1967
5455	Welborn, Suma F.		
		Sam N. Welborn	12 Jan. 1965
6787	Welch, Walter G.		
		Sue H. Welch	23 May 1977
5632	Welcott, Cynthia Marie		
		Chas. Ray Welcott	25 Feb. 1966
4637	Wellborn, Robert M.		
		Berlyn Jean	6 Oct. 1931
79153a	Wells, Linda Lea		
		James Dowling Wells	4 Oct. 1979
8780a	Wells, Sherman T. Jr.		
		Barbara J. Wells	24 June 1987
2805	Welsh, James L.		
		Estella Welsh	10 Dec. 1945
79213a	Welsh, John Brent		
		Mary Louise Welsh	20 May 1980
82224a	Welsh, Mary Gale		
		John Brent Welsh	4 Apr. 1983
3882	Welty, Emogene Elois		
		Lawrence Welty	15 Dec. 1952
85101a	Welty, Glenda J.		
		Larry W. Welty	28 Aug. 1985
3280	Welty, Lawrence		
		Dorothy Welty	25 Oct. 1948
88197a	Welty, Leta Jane		
		Peter Cash Welty	22 Feb. 1981
81211a	Welwood, Bett Jo		
		Richard L. Welwood	4 Feb. 1982
3991	Wengenroth, Anna Jo		
		Gilbert Wengenroth	9 Sept. 1953
1779	Wescott, Grace		
		Mark Wescott	20 Mar. 1933
2653	Wesley, Mary Lee		
		Albert Wesley	24 Mar. 1944

Case	Plaintiff	Defendant	Date
4902	West, Nancy Dorene		
		William R. West Jr.	12 Apr. 1961
6978	Weyland, Chas. Quinlan		
		Elsie Fern Weyland	23 Sug. 1978
2219	Wharton, Emily E.		
		Newton Wharton	20 Sept. 1938
4576	Wheat, Mary Jane		
		Wm. Arthur Wheat	1 Apr. 1958
1939	Wheat, Saddie		
		Will A. Wheat	15 Apr. 1936
82229a	Wheatley, Barbara Sue		
		Richard Duncan Wheatley	6 Apr. 1983
2682	Wheatley, Dorothy		
		Clifford Wheatley	6 Dec. 1943
3640	Wheeler, Lillian		
		David Richard Wheeler	17 Apr. 1952
1879	Wheelus, Minnie Mae		
		Cleve Wheelus	9 Oct. 1934
2069	Wheelus, Ruth		
		Cleve Wheelus	13 Oct. 1936
2440	Whisenhunt, Gladys		
		Roy Whisenhunt	16 Sept. 1940
80219a	White, Barbara Ann		
		Lynn Vernon White	19 Oct. 1981
84249a	White, Dorothy Virginia		
		James Russell White	27 Dec. 1984
86019a	White, Gerald A.		
		Lucilla Lopez White	1 Aug. 1986
87115a	White, Gerald A.		
		Lucilla Lopez White	21 Oct. 1987
3708	White, J. H.		
		Pearl Viola White	25 Sept. 1951
5094	White, Maxine K.		
		William M. White	25 Apr. 1962
8056a	White, Patrick Burton		
		Gabrielle Fraenkel White	
			18 June 1980
4828	White, Stanley Jr.		
		Mary Inez White	5 Feb. 1960
3599	White, Viola		
		Virgil White	25 May 1951
80241a	White, Willie Doris		
		Gerald Anthony White	2 Jan 1981

Case	Plaintiff / Defendant	Date
1594	Whitfield, A. G.	
	Helena Whitfield	22 Apr. 1931
5441	Whitmore, Patricia Vonne	
	Russell Dale Whitmore	1 June 1965
84	Whittbold, Henry	
	Wilhelmine Whittbold	20 Sept. 1878
4257	Whitted, Wynonna J. N.	
	Wm. Howard Whitted	22 Sept. 1955
8850a	Whitton, Katherine J.	
	Burin J. Whitten Jr.	18 May 1988
2860	Whitwood, Velma	
	Lawrence Whitwood	8 Oct. 1945
4662	Whorton, Dorothy Lee	
	George Clay Whorton	28 Oct. 1958
84201a	Wickcliffe, Alma Nell	
	Bobby Glenn Wickcliff	23 May 1985
4026	Wickson, Earleen	
	Prentice D. Wickson	17 Dec. 1953
4030	Wickson, Mary K.	
	Lonnie D. Wickson	2 Feb. 1954
5698	Wideman, Frances W.	
	Henry L. Wideman Jr.	7 July 1966
5246	Wiecking, Emmadell S.	
	Herman A. Wiecking	8 Jan. 1964
87233a	Wiese, Walter Clifford	
	Larrisa Crenshaw Wiese	3 Dec. 1987
86224a	Wilbanks, Elizabeth Jo	
	Wm. Arnold Wilbanks	5 Nov. 1986
4658	Wilhelm, Hattie	
	Zilmer T. Wilhelm	14 Oct. 1958
5770	Wilke, Eugene M.	
	Helen F. Wilke	28 Oct. 1966
5843	Wilke, Patty	
	Donald Wilke	17 Apr. 1967
1942	Wilkerson, Steve O.	
	Mary Ellen Wilkerson	21 Oct. 1935
3419	Wilkinson, Dorothy	
	Sam G. Wilkinson	6 Sept. 1949
5868	Wilkinson, Dorothy Ann	
	Archie Wilkinson	23 May 1967
2516	Wilkinson, Mabel	
	Sam G. Wilkinson	2 Oct. 1941
3641	Wilkinson, Sam G.	
	Dorothy M. Wilkinson	26 Apr. 1951

Case	Plaintiff	Defendant	Date
5124	Williams, Arnold		
		Bobbie Laura Williams	23 July 1962
8812a	Williams, Barney Keith		
		Kari Lee Williams	5 Aug. 1988
80232a	Williams, Billy Howard		
		Agnes Theresa Wilson	5 Mar. 1981
5299	Williams, Bruce		
		Frances Petty Williams	20 Mar. 1964
4840	Williams, Donald L.		
		Jo Ann Williams	30 Apr. 1960
2344	Williams, Jas. T.		
		Lucy B. Williams	19 Sept. 1939
78146a	Williams, Joe T.		
		Aileen Baker Williams	2 May 1979
3877	Williams, June Eileen		
		Jesse Thos. Williams	11 Feb. 1953
4109	Williams, Lorena Jolene		
		Theron Marvin Williams	7 Sept. 1954
78105a	Williams, Louis Henry		
		Zanna Mae Valerie Williams	
			16 Jan. 1979
8144a	Williams, Louis Henry		
		Mary Sue Sutton Williams	
			30 Nov. 1981
2958	Williams, Marshall B.		
		Frances Williams	22 Apr. 1946
3565	Williams, Martha		
		Fred Williams	28 Nov. 1950
82250a	Williams, Michelle Marie		
		Jeffery Williams	3 Feb. 1983
5018	Williams, Patricia		
		Earlie Williams Jr.	13 May 1963
5869	Williams, Patricia Jo		
		Billie Howard Williams	6 Oct. 1967
3620	Williams, Patsy		
		Gene Williams	15 Dec. 1952
9554a	Williams, Ruby Ann		
		Robert E. Williams	23 May 1985
1593	Williams, Sadie		
		J. T. Williams	2 Apr. 1931
84308a	Williams, Thomas J.		
		Nellie Faye Williams	9 Jan. 1985
2798	Williams, Tillie		
		Bruce Williams	25 May 1945

Case	Plaintiff	Defendant	Date
86241a	Williams, Vanessa Jean		
		Earlie Williams III 1	10 Feb. 1988
2479	Williams, W. W.		
		Lera Ruth Williams	17 Mar. 1941
4954	Williams, Wanda Lucille		
		Walter Scott Williams	12 Mar. 1963
79140a	Williamson, Betty Jane		
		Malcomb Colan Williamson	19 Oct. 1979
3297	Williamson, Carley J.		
		Eula L. Williamson	9 Sept. 1948
6222	Williamson, Thomas Joe		
		Clarice Mildred Williamson	12 Feb. 1970
2624	Willis, Clay E.		
		Florence A. Willis	23 Mar. 1943
6038	Willis, Damon D.		
		Sherry B. Willis	6 Jan. 1989
4728	Willis, Vivian		
		W. P. Willis	18 Apr. 1959
6307	Willis, Willian D.		
		Joyce M. Willis	5 Nov. 1969
80157a	Wilmeth, Susie Neily		
		Ross Alton Wilmeth	11 Sept. 1980
1754	Wilson, Andy		
		Fern Wilson	9 Oct. 1933
5193	Wilson, Betty Jane		
		John H. Wilson	13 May 1963
84234a	Wilson, Darla Kay		
		Richard Wayne Wilson	29 Oct. 1984
3372	Wilson, Dora		
		Anthony D. Wilson	23 May 1949
4706	Wilson Ella Irene		
		Richard Clay Wilson	4 July 1959
4754	Wilson, Farrell		
		Wayne Wilson	24 July 1959
1674	Wilson, Fern		
		Andy Wilson	22 Oct. 1932
4501	Wilson, Frances		
		Job Wilson	26 Aug. 1957
2872	Wilson, Grace		
		Jessie M. Wilson	13 Nov. 1945
4942	Wilson, James A.		
		Daisy Inez Wilson	3 Jan. 1961
80207a	Wilson Janice W.		
		Larry W. Wilson	19 June 1981

139

Case	Plaintiff	Defendant	Date
4001	Wilson, Jesse Melvin		
		Vivian G. Wilson	2 Feb. 1954
5482	Wilson, Mack David		
		Merry Linda Wilson	9 Apr. 1965
6328	Wilson, Mack David		
		Gwendolyn Yvonne Wilson	21 Nov. 1069
3723	Wilson, Mary Peschel		
		M. W. Wilson	8 Nov. 1951
1758	Wilson, Melvin		
		Franque Wilson	19 Apr. 1933
2159	Wilson, Melvin		
		Gladys V. Wilson	4 Oct. 1937
6261	Wilson. Patricia C.		
		Lloyd H. Wilson	24 July 1969
5480	Wilson, Phyllis		
		Lee Wilson	19 Mar. 1965
2892	Wilson, R. C.		
		Tommye Wilson	10 Dec. 1945
1849	Wilson, Robert I.		
		Marjorie Wilson	16 June 1934
4793	Wilson, Ruth T.		
		Albert S. Wilson	5 June 1961
852a	Wilson, Sandra Sue		
		Michael Len Wilson	6 Mar. 1985
5995	Wilson, Shirley		
		Carol Leon Wilson	18 Oct. 1968
83188a	Wilson, Teresa Alana		
		Bobby Joe Wilson	28 Oct. 1983
2591	Wilson, Theo		
		Walter Elmo Wilson	30 Apr. 1942
8512a	Wilson, Tomas W.		
		Vicky L. Wilson	9 Apr. 1985
4896	Wilton, Jerry A.		
		Peggy Lynn Wilton	16 Sept. 1960
5075	Wilton, J. R.		
		Dorothy Wilton	15 July 1963
5128	Winskey, Claudia Dell		
		Gordon Thos. Winskey	20 Aug. 1962
8850a	Winston, Bert F. Jr.		
		Beverly S. Winston	27 June 1989
80196a	Wixson, Cheryl Ann		
		William Evert Wixson	31 Dec. 1980
4538	Woerner, Eugenia Susan		
		Kermit W. Woerner	26 Apr. 1957

Case	Plaintiff	Defendant	Date
5175	Wolfe, Tommie D.		
		Russell S. Wolfe	6 Mar. 1963
3807	Womack, Dorothy		
		Mark C. Womack	2 Sept. 1952
82251a	Wood, Claud Charles		
		Margaret Ann Wood	21 Jan. 1983
6303	Wood, Fay		
		Theodore Jackson Wood	11 Dec. 1969
6266	Wood, Ida Jewel		
		Harold T. Wood	29 July 1969
82101a	Wood, Joseph W.		
		Debra M. Wood	30 Aug. 1982
1774	Wood, Pauline		
		Dayton Wood	19 Apr. 1933
79130a	Woodard, Nevada L.		
		Harlen J. Woodard	13 Sept. 1939
82141a	Woodbridge, Barbara Lange		
		William Douglas Woodbridge Jr.	8 Oct. 1982
2624	Woods, Jesse G.		
		Gertrude Woods	9 Mar. 1942
5125	Woods, John C.		
		Betty Jo Woods	7 Jan. 1963
3270	Woods, Willie		
		Olidia H. Woods	8 Sept. 1948
1755	Woods, William Hariet		
		Octavia Bailey Woods	28 Oct. 1933
8645a	Woolbridge, Betsy Englemon		
		Chas. Ray Woolbridge	13 May 1986
85123a	Woolls, Eva Ellen		
		Richard Earl Woolls	31 July 1985
2273	Wooton, G. A.		
		Jessie Wooton	19 Sept. 1939
2996	Wooton, Louie		
		Pearl Wooton	22 July 1946
85288a	Worsham, Robert Allen		
		Mary Lee Worsham	1 Aug. 1986
6320	Worthy, Ludie Marie		
		William Ray Worthy	26 July 1973
4328	Wren, Beatrice		
		Lee Wren	13 Sept. 1956
5307	Wren, Elizabeth Weaver		
		Elmer E. Wren	11 May 1964

Case	Plaintiff	Defendant	Date
4810	Wren, Elmer Earl		
		Dixie Lee Wren	29 Feb. 1960
4350	Wright, Ann		
		Jack Wright	14 July 1956
2024	Wright, Beatrice		
		J. W. Wright	21 Apr. 1936
5604	Wright, Chester		
		Elsie McMahon Wright	22 Dec. 1965
6211	Wright, Chester		
		Edna E. Wright	27 May 1969
82136a	Wright, Jack N.		
		Ruby Lee Wright	5 May 1983
3646	Wright, Jessie E.		
		Capt. H. E. Wright	24 Apr. 1951
2924	Wright, Rosaline		
		Ernest Wright	4 Mar. 1948
6329	Weight, Viola		
		Jack M. Wright	23 Dec. 1969
5571	Wroe, Clifton W.		
		Nellie Katherine Wroe	6 Oct. 1977
8671a	Wuest, Laura Belinda		
		Michael James Wuest	29 Aug. 1986
4408	Wyatt, Carolyn		
		Harmon Lee Wyatt	18 Feb. 1957
82107a	Wylds, Tracy Lynn		
		Michael Troy Wylds	22 Oct. 1982

X

NONE

Y

Case	Plaintiff	Defendant	Date
8530a	Yancey, Charles Emerson		
		Sarah Frances Yancey	9 Apr. 1985
2279	Yarber, Alta		
		Melvin Yarber	10 Mar. 1939
3840	Yarborough, Tallie Mae		
		Pleasant W. Yarborough	12 Sept. 1952
4260	Yarborough, Tallie Mae		
		Pleasant W. Yarborough	22 Nov. 1955

Case	Plaintiff	Defendant	Date
81145a	Yarbrough, Victoria Marie		
		Reuel Wayne Yarbrough	30 Sept. 1981
81255a	Yarbrough, Virginia Ruth		
		Don Allan Yarbrough	24 Feb. 1982
2825	Yardley, Eva Mae		
		Doyle R. Yardley	6 July 1945
3333	Ybarra, Porfirio		
		Antonio G. Ybarra	7 Feb. 1949
82135a	Ybarra, Rosemary Rodriguez		
		Florencio Ybarra	15 Nov. 1982
8830a	Yeager, Sherry Kim		
		Henry Christopher Yeager	5 May 1988
6158	York, Robert C.		
		Billy Jean York	9 Dec. 1968
8258a	York, Ronald Keith		
		Linda Kathleen York	6 July 1982
2861	York, Thelma E.		
		Robert A. York Jr.	3 Nov. 1945
5333	Young, Ada		
		James T. Young Jr.	29 May 1964
80153a	Young, Bobby Don		
		Maureen Ann Young	15 Dec. 1980
3187	Young, Jessie		
		William Young	6 Feb. 1950
4323	Young, Marvin R.		
		Dorothy Pauline Young	14 May 1956
2059	Young, Mattie		
		Ralph Young	9 Oct. 1936
83246a	Young, Miriam Chambers		
		John Edwin Young	24 Feb. 1984
2416	Young, Odele S.		
		James T. Young	19 Sept. 1940
8265a	Young, Phillis Ann		
		Ronald Don Young	8 Oct. 1982
2467	Youngblood, Lillie M.		
		George Youngblood	25 Mar. 1941
3618	Youngblood, Lillie Mae		
		George J. Youngblood	18 June 1951

Z

Case	Plaintiff	Defendant	Date
81176a	Zeinner, Frederick Joseph		
		Bonnie Jean Edson Zeinner	
			20 Oct. 1981
81232a	Zell, Tina Ann		
		Jeffery Frank Zell	5 Dec. 1984
5056	Zuspann, Dorothy Sublett		
		Leslie Zuspann	12 Mar. 1962

Case	Plaintiff	Defendant	Date

A

88115a	Abbott, Gracie Lexie		
		Carroll Tex Abbott	19 Aug. 1988
8660a	Abbott, Jeanne		
		Carroll Mark Abbott	7 July 1986
86108a	Abernathy, Michael Eugene		
		Jo Ann Abernathy	11 June 1988
86227b	Abshier, John Acy		
		Gail Lynn Abshier	21 Jan. 1987
90291b	Abshier, John Acy		
		Louise Sewell Conroy	11 July 1990
88186a	Acevedo, Lucy Lopez		
		Avelino DeLa Paz	13 Sept. 1989
CV88178	Acker, Marsha Renee		
		Thomas Allen Acker	22 Dec. 1988
88243b	Adams, Pricilla K.		
		Joseph P. Adams	5 Apr. 1989
86172a	Adams, Timothy Lee		
		Stephanie Adams	15 Oct. 1986
8989b	Adamson, Barbara Jane		
		Monroe Adamson	6 Apr. 1990
89130b	Aguilar, Natividad G.		
		Joe L. Aguilar	6 June 1998
8987c	Aguirre, Debra		
		Reyes Aguirre	13 July 1989
CV87273	Aherns, Emma Rosalie		
		Allen Arthur Aherns	28 Dec. 1987
87136b	Alese, Carol Jo		
		Anthony Alese	10 Sept. 1987
CV87313	Alesee, Anthony		
		Carol Jo Alesee	25 Feb. 1988
89140a	Alexander, Jamesine		
		Benny Dewayne Alexander	4 Oct. 1989
90291b	Alishier, John Acy		
		Louise Sewell Conroy Alisher	
			11 July 1990
CV86226	Allen, Edna Benson		
		Jerry Allen Sr.	7 Jan 1987
89251b	Allen, Michael L.		
		Vickie Lynn G. Allen	5 Mar. 1990

145

Case	Plaintiff	Defendant	Date
89198a	Allen, Patricia Ann		
		Larry Lynn Allen	17 Nov. 1989
Cv88255	Allen Rita J.		
		Sammy John Allen	20 Dec. 1988
8979b	Anbunathan, Snela Pradan		
		Beryl Jeganter Davidson	23 Aug. 1989
8930c	Anderson, Karen S.		
		Thomas Anderson	19 Apr. 1989
CV87280	Anderson, Ora Katherine		
		William K. Anderson	29 Mar. 1987
88278b	Angell, Richard James		
		Meta Louise Angell	18 Oct. 1989
8977c	Anguiano, Kelli Ann		
		Leroy Anguiano	5 July 1989
88203a	Appling, Alice Ann		
		Van Jon Appling	13 Jan. 1987
CV86153	Arp, Judi Marie		
		Billy Joe Arp	25 July 1986
8882a	Arreola, Ascuncien Martinez		
		Manuel Arreola	6 July 1988
CV88226	Arreola, Guadalupe Ramirez Jr.		
		Eunice Aguilar Arreola	16 Dec. 1988
CV86123	Arredondo, Oscar		
		Adlina Arredondo	20 June 1986
89265	Asbrock, George C.		
		Wanda Mae Asbrock	11 Apr. 1990
89292b	Ashcraft, Debra Sue S.		
		Clinton Eric Ashcraft	28 Mar. 1990
CV8855	Atkinson, Joe Marshall		
		Mollie Hudeck Atkinson	3 Aug. 1988
CV88239	Avery, Homer James		
		Carmen Martinez Avery	11 Jan. 1990
87216a	Ayala, Blanca Alicia W.		
		Gilbert Calderon Ayala	19 Nov. 1987
89265b	Ayala, Josephine Castillo		
		Regino Gene Ayala	28 Feb, 1990
89200b	Ayala, Olga May		
		Reymundo Ayala	20 Dec. 1989

B

CV87307	Babb, Nancy L.		
		Gary D. Babb	5 Feb. 1988

Case	Plaintiff	Defendant	Date
88233a	Bacilieri, Stephen Gary		
		Jean Rogers Bacilieri	14 Mar. 1990
CV8641	Bacon, Sidney Berry		
		Dan Wallace Bacon	8 July 1986
90240c	Baethge, Arnell Beatrice		
		Gregory Lynn Baethge	23 July 1990
CV8592	Bailey, Jerry Don		
		Barbara Jane Bailey	26 Feb. 1987
CV86179	Baker, Diane		
		Kenneth Martin Baker	16 Apr. 1987
CV86320	Balderama, Arturo		
		Nativida Balderama	23 Dec. 1986
90233a	Balderama, Arturo		
		Margie Auld Balderama	26 Sept. 1990
890215a	Ballesteros, Florinda Torres		
		Greg Ballesteros	31 Jan. 1990
90329b	Barbosa, Carmela		
		Antonio Barbosa	11 Aug. 1990
90236a	Barnett, Peter J.		
		Linda A. Harmon Barnett	11 June 1990
8948c	Barrowman, Ella Burgess		
		George E. Barrowman	24 May 1989
CV87152	Bartell, Mark Gillis		
		Sharon Kay Vaughn Bartell	
			6 Oct. 1987
CV8819	Barton, Jesse Lee		
		Mary Alice Barton	29 Mar. 1988
CV87260	Bascom, Ralph G.		
		Connie M. Bascom	15 Dec. 1987
89143b	Basse, Lori Jean		
		James Michael Basse	5 Apr. 1990
90241c	Bates, Billy P.		
		Marilyn Faye Bates	10 July 1990
CV87168	Battean, Rosaline Delores		
		Robert Charles Battean	16 Sept. 1988
89143b	Baxter, Tamara Woerner		
		Rodney Baxter	21 Nov, 1989
CV88229	Beadles, Hugh Alan		
		Judy Jean Beadles	29 Nov. 1988
CV8783	Becker, Kandy Kukendall		
		Kenneth Wayne Becker	15 July 1987
CV86258	Beach, Thonda Adams		
		Timothy Allan Beach	17 Nov. 1986

Case	Plaintiff	Defendant	Date
CV88258	Beakley, Martha Jane		
		Billy Jack Beakley	24 May 1989
CV87289	Beall, Ruth H.		
		Daniel Elbert Beall	17 Mar. 1989
8911b	Beaver, Bobbie Allanor		
		Robert Russell Beaver	5 Jan. 1989
89200a	Bebee, Gina Ann		
		David Ray Bebee	25 Jan. 1990
CV87284	Bell, Dana Joan		
		Rance Carlton Bell	5 Jan. 1988
CV86229	Bell, Sherry Lee		
		Herbert Ralph Bell Jr.	3 Dec. 1986
90283B	Benfer, Robert Leon		
		Janeese Benfer	10 Oct. 1990
CV86363	Benitez, Eloe		
		Pamela Gayle Benitez	20 May 1987
CV86293	Benjamin, Daniel Alan		
		Sara Lynn Benjamin	7 Jan. 1987
89170b	Benson, Rita Gayle		
		William A. Benson	14 Feb. 1990
9048c	Berlingeri, Andrew Dominic		
		Lorna Jan Berlingeri	9 Apr. 1990
CV859	Bevers, Bill		
		Norma E. Bevers	11 Dec. 1985
90576b	Bierman, Joseph M.		
		Lisa M. Bierman	12 Dec. 1990
89113c	Biermann, Carl E.		
		Elaine E. Biermann	9 Aug. 1989
CV86264	Biernat, Linda Carol		
		Walter Stanley Biernat	29 Dec. 1968
89199b	Blondkeim, Rosalind F.		
		William Blondkeim	27 Aug. 1990
CV85124	Bogotchow, Lynn Marie		
		Roman Bogotchow	12 Mar. 1986
Cv8755	Boni, Bethyn Ann		
		Steven Dwayne Boni	26 May 1987
8926c	Booth, Mabel Clair Tonneson		
		Kenneth Vance Booth	19 Apr. 1989
90235c	Bowlin, Glenna J.		
		Michael R. Bowlin	6 June 1990
CV8699	Britsch, Elroy C.		
		Peggy A. Britsch	5 June 1986
CV8613	Brodie, Caroly Elaine		
		James Robert Brodie Jr.	26 Mar. 1986

Case	Plaintiff	Defendant	Date
CV88270	Brondo, Aracely		
		Ronnie Brondo	30 Jan. 1989
CV8724	Bronson, James Phillip		
		Cleo Ruth Bronson	13 May 1987
89229a	Brown, Donna Renee		
		Ronald A. Brown	16 Feb. 1990
CV187	Brown, Rosemary		
		James Mack Brown	4 Oct. 1988
89136c	Browning, Linda Clay		
		Joe B. Browning	9 Apr. 1990
CV87203	Buck, Robert Edward		
		Robin Lynn Buck	24 Nov. 1987
9064a	Buckner, Dennis		
		Elaine L. Buckner	18 May 1990
90171c	Burdette, Sonja Dee		
		William Jerry Burdette	18 June 1990
8943c	Burgassier, Bernadette A.		
		Robert B. Burgassier	7 June 1989
CV85161	Burgess, Peggy Lynn		
		Billy Bob Burgess	31 Jan. 1986
CV85250	Burleson, Rebecca Nell		
		Joseph Burton Burleson	20 Feb. 1986
CV8770	Burney, Sammy J.		
		Patricia A. Burney	1 June 1987
CV88273	Burns, Nancy		
		Patrick Kevin Burns	16 Nov. 1989
90106a	Burton, Roland T.		
		Marionette Mullins Burton	6 June 1990
CV7257	Bush, Barbara Ann		
		Leamon Edward Bush	12 Apr. 1988
90235c	Bynum, Sandra		
		Dennis Bynum	3 Oct. 1990
CV8843	Byrd, Teddy Urban		
		Glenda S. Byrd	27 Apr. 1988

C

8946c	Cade, Colleen Bryant		
		Robert Bernard Cade Jr.	28 July 1989
CV86174	Calderon, Petra Eliza		
		Homero Calderon	9 Dec. 1989

Case	Plaintiff	Defendant	Date
CV86207	Callahan, Lana Lee Raodein		
		William Paul Callahan	16 Oct. 1986
CV86359	Calvin, Chris W.		
		Phyllis F. Calvin	25 Feb. 1987
CV855	Cantino, Sylvia Garza		
		John Islas Cantino	15 Jan 1986
89107a	Cantwell, Richard D.		
		Connie Renee Le Sturgeon Cantwell	14 Aug. 1989
89168c	Caracciola, Cynthia Ann		
		Louis Edward Caracciola	16 Oct. 1989
CV86358	Carrales, Patricia A.		
		Ricardo M. Carrales	2 Apr. 1987
89108a	Cepeda, Edna Jo		
		Jose Cepeda	18 Sept, 1989
90337c	Chacon, Brenda Gay		
		Steven E. Chacon	15 Aug. 1990
89170a	Chacon, Pennelope Carr		
		Rudy Chacon	5 Nov. 1990
CV857	Chandler, Tray Lynne		
		Wilson Jerome Chandler	18 Dec. 1985
CV8511	Charnichart, Jacob		
		Constance Charnichart	19 Mar. 1986
9027c	Chevalier, Fayee Lanette Freeman		
		Clinton David Chevalier	28 Mar. 1990
CV8595	Chicowske, Albert M.		
		Helen S. Chicowske	20 Feb. 1986
896b	Childers, Erie R.		
		William Michael Childers	5 Apr. 1989
CV85229	Chomout, Sandra Kay		
		Steven Anthony Chomout	7 Apr. 1985
CV85249	Cina, Ronald Anthony		
		Prisciella Lee Cina	19 Feb. 1986
89168b	Clemer, Judith Squibble		
		Michael Craig Clemer	25 Oct. 1989
CV8655	Cluck, Darrell Wayne		
		Katherine Eliz. Cluck	22 Apr. 1986
CV86157	Colbath, James B.		
		Shana M. Colbath	19 Oct. 1986
90115b	Collier, Sheila Kay		
		Steven Jesse Collier Jr.	20 June 1990
CV86267	Collier, Steven Jessie		
		Ethel Elizabeth Collier	7 Jan. 1987

Case	Plaintiff	Defendant	Date
89160a	Constante, Nancy A.		
		William L. Constante	5 Oct. 1989
CV85115	Cooper, Joe A.		
		Dorothy M. Cooper	4 Feb. 1986
90367c	Council, Deeandra K.		
		Anthony M. Council	14 Nov. 1990
8954c	Council, Pamela I.		
		Cody Don Council	30 Aug. 1989
CV88146	Cox, Betty Mahan		
		John David Cox	6 Feb. 1989
CV8711	Cremin, Carol Underwood		
		Walter C. J. Cremin	1 Apr. 1987
8949a	Crews, Harriett Saunders		
		Caray W. Crews	11 Aug. 1989
89111c	Crider, Roy Matthew		
		Sherry Lynn Crider	31 Aug. 1989
CV85121	Crider, Susan Gay		
		James Robert Crider	22 Jan 1986
89171B	Crider, Thad James		
		Kelly Ann Crider	25 Oct. 1989
90455c	Crites, Jamey Lynette		
		Steven Wayne Crites	26 Sept. 1990
CV88164	Crites, Christine Kay		
		Curtis Jay Crites	1 Dec. 1988
CV86191	Croft, James Donald		
		Sherrylene Parry Croft	2 Sept. 1986
90116	Crooks, Patsy Kay		
		Ronald Albert Crooks II	2 May 1990
90212c	Crowley, Delia		
		Daniel Allen Crowley	6 June 1990
89235b	Cruz, Felipa Alverez		
		Lorenzo Rodriguez Cruz	20 Apr. 1990
89154a	Cushman, Brenda Carol		
		Robert Willis	17 Nov. 1989

D

Case	Plaintiff	Defendant	Date
89281b	Damron, Mary A.		
		Stanley D. Damron	31 May 1990
909c	Davila, Silvia Garcia		
		Juan Lorenzo	14 May 1990
CV87287	Davis, Allison F.		
		Gary L. Davis	21 Jan. 1988

Case	Plaintiff	Defendant	Date
89233b	Davis, Doris		
		Osrel Davis	23 Jan. 1990
CV88214	Deike, Krista Adele		
		Daron Clay Deike	23 May 1987
8974b	Dela Cruz, Jo Ann		
		Larry Dela Cruz	20 Sept. 1990
8974b	De La Rosa, Marie E.		
		Isidero De La Rosa	11 July 1989
CV87272	DeLeon, Elam		
		Steve DeLeon	3 Nov. 1988
89136b	Delesdernier, Lucretia A.		
		James M. Delesdernier	4 Oct. 1989
8970a	Delgadillo, Isabel Lopez		
		Daniel R. Delgadillo	9 Aug. 1989
89265c	Delgado, Randisue		
		Fernando J. Delgado	3 Dec. 1990
CV88167	DeLong, Brenda		
		David Allan DeLong	9 Nov. 1988
CV86192	Denman, Kester Walker III		
		Joyce Elaine Denman	3 Oct. 1986
89229b	Derowen, Alicia K.		
		Brian K. Derowen Sr.	3 Apr. 1990
8977b	Derrick, Ronald Allen		
		Margaret Denise Derrick	9 Aug, 1989
89-41c	Dewey, Merlene G.		
		Richard K. Dewey Jr.	3 May 1989
90519c	Dietert, Amy Diane		
		Stephen Wm. Dietert	28 Nov. 1990
CV8791	Dietert, Stephen William		
		Marsha Gwenel Dietert	21 Aug. 1987
CV86309	Dion, Sherri L Cowait		
		Carey Joseph Dion	30 Dec. 1986
CV87329	Donaghe, Austin Wayne		
		Vaneta Donaghe	10 Mar. 1988
CV86233	Donald, Athena Jean		
		Jimmy Dale Donald	30 Jan. 1987
CV8714	Donaldson, Julie S.		
		David Alan Donaldson	8 May 1987
CV88284	Donato, Sandra J.		
		Michael A. Donato	19 June 1989
CV85242	Dorsett, Robbie Raye		
		Wade Oran Dorsett	12 Mar. 1986
CV86142	Downey, Debra L.		
		James L. Downey	7 July 1986

Case	Plaintiff	Defendant	Date
CV8584	Dozier, Diane		
	John Clifton Dozier		12 Dec. 1985
CV86101	Dozier, James M.		
	Linda D. Simmons Dozier		4 June 1986
89195a	Duhr, Nicole Andrea		
	Jacques Gaston Duhr		6 Dec. 1989
89233a	Dukarm, Michelle		
	Donald Dwayne Dukarm		17 Jan 1990
8892b	Duncan, Marcella B.		
	Marion E. Duncan		18 July 1989
90263b	Dyal, Thomas L.		
	Maryellen Dyal		5 July 1990
90344b	Dye, Jessica M.		
	David Wade Dye III		22 Oct. 1990

E

Case	Plaintiff	Defendant	Date
8969c	Edwards, Collene Lee		
	Martin Lynn Edwards		10 July 1989
CV8515	Edwards, Florence		
	Aubrey Edwards		20 Dec. 1985
89140b	Edwards. Suzanne S.		
	John R. Edwards		4 Jan. 1990
8993a	Elliott, Serena Ann		
	Clayton Dean Elliott		1 Aug. 1990
90328c	Emerson, Norman Dale		
	Sharon Lee Emerson		29 July 1990
8955c	Ersch, Mary Louise		
	Gene Alex Ersch		2 July 1989
8992a	Espinoza, Tony Moreno		
	Martha Rodriguez Espinoza		17 Jan. 1990
CV8861	Estrada, Rosie M.		
	Enrique Estrada		10 Jan 1989
CV86344	Evans, Annie Mae		
	Lemuel/Samuel Evans		10 Feb. 1987
CV88317	Evans, Jimmie Lewis		
	Barbara Graham Evans		8 Mar. 1988

F

Case	Plaintiff	Defendant	Date
CV8629	Ficker, Charles Michael		
		Deanne Deidra Ficker	2 Apr. 1986
CV87195	Fields, Evangelina Aleman		
		Harry Bole Fields III	7 Oct. 1987
8917b	Fikes, Ann L.		
		Robert Ray Fikes	6 Dec. 1980
90517c	Fisher, Corina Jane		
		Edward Doss Fisher	19 Nov. 1990
90328b	Fisher, Sharon Ann Larkin		
		Billy Fisher	20 Dec. 1990
CV86329	Flaherity Rebecca Lee		
		Daniel Everett Flaherity	23 June 1989
89146c	Flanagan, Allison Gehle		
		Michael Scott Flanagan	11 July 1990
89201c	Fleming, Harry L. III		
		Joyce Ann Fleming	28 Feb. 1990
CV8676	Fletcher, Cynthia Ann		
		Charles Wm. Fletcher Jr.	19 May 1986
CV87316	Flood, Charles Martin		
		Shirley Kennedy Flood	3 Oct. 1988
CV86251	Flores, Martin De Leon		
		Teresa Gaye Flores	8 May 1987
89105a	Flores, Sylvia Ledezma		
		Ismael Garza Flores	6 Oct. 1989
90148c	Floyd, Janice		
		William E. Floyd	19 May 1990
89104a	Foster, Brenda		
		Noah Allen Foster	23 Oct. 1989
CV8632	Foster, Clifton Burl		
		Belinda Elaine Foster	23 Jan. 1987
Cv87197	Foster, Robert John		
		Judy Kay Foster	4 Jan 1988
CV86173	Foster, Wanda Geraldine		
		Charles J. Foster	17 Dec. 1986
CV86189	Frandin, Jane Britt Williams		
		Carl George Frandin	13 Aug. 1986
9030c	Frausto, Eva Gonzales		
		John Moses Frausto	28 Mar. 1990

G

CV8744	Gafford, Eddie Jean		
		Marvin Gafford	5 May 1989

Case	Plaintiff	Defendant	Date

CV86210 Gage, Dale Neilsen
        Tommy Gage   21 Jan. 1987

CV88113 Garcia, Casildo
        Josepha Garcia   5 Sept. 1989

CV88310 Garcia, Cynthia Ann
        Raul Garcia   13 Mar. 1989

CV8833 Garcia, Mary Gale
        Placido Garcia   14 Apr. 1980

CV88287 Garnett, Wyatt Dean
        Martha Vickie Barton Garnett
                         31 Oct. 1989

8924b Gay, Cloie Elaine
        Wayne Robin Gay   5 Apr. 1989

90591c Garza, David
        Thelma Garza   21 Dec. 1990

89275a Garza, Debra Lee
        Carlos G. Garza   12 Mar. 1990

CV88202 Garza, Joseph J.
        Maria Guadalupe Garcia 29 Nov. 1988

90267b Garza, Julie Natividad
        Christopher Gene Garza 23 May 1990

CV356 Garza, Kim Susan
        Richard J. Garza   2 Mar. 1987

CV276 Gauthrie, Betty Jeanette
        Ricky Eugene Gauthrie 30 Nov. 1987

CV86116 Gerdemon, Susan E.
        James Gerdemon   30 Dec. 1986

CV8644 Gerstenberg, Gilbert A. III
        Roberta D. Gerstenberg 27 Mar, 1986

89161a Gillum, David L.
        Jennifer L. Gillum   4 Oct. 1989

CV86132 Gingrich, Dzintra Milda Salme
        Alan Ray Gingrich   11 May 1987

CV87275 Goetz, Marsha Joann
        Richard Frederick Goetz
                         23 Dec. 1987

8911a Gomez, Diane Lavern
        Bulerno Graham   15 Mar. 1989

8928c Gonzales, Elana Christine
        Frank Diaz Gonzales 17 Apr. 1989

90268a Goodman, Theresa Yvonne
        Steve Patrick Goodman 14 Nov. 1990

CV8677 Goulden, Gerald W.
        Laura Jo Ann Goulden 18 May 1986

Case	Plaintiff	Defendant	Date
89273b	Gradoville, Jean		
		Edwin John Gradoville	2 Apr. 1990
CV8924a	Graham, David Austin		
		Sylvia Kraft Graham	5 Apr. 1989
89106a	Graham, Peggy Sue Nelson		
		Gary Ray Graham	31 July 1989
CV8825	Gray, Douglas Wayne		
		Tommy Lynn Gray	26 Sept. 1988
90361b	Green, Denice Irene		
		Thomas William Green	15 Aug. 1990
90392c	Green, Leigh Jeffers		
		Britton Curtis Green	15 Aug. 1990
CV8836	Green Rosetta		
		John Raymond Green	1 June 1988
CV86287	Green, Sherron Kay		
		Alan Miles Green	3 Dec. 1986
89154a	Greer, Carol Anne		
		Dillard Lee Greer	10 Oct. 1989
CV88155	Grier, Cassandra Gaye		
		Larry Frank Grier	7 Apr. 1989
90380c	Griffin, Richard Dale		
		Laura Leigh Griffin	10 Aug. 1990
90285b	Groll, Donna M.		
		Dale A. Groll	19 Dec. 1990
8955a	Grumbles, Glenn D.		
		Gloria D. Grumbles	7 June 1989
89260b	Guerra, Michael		
		Evelyn Tyson Guerra	31 Jan. 1990
CV86197	Guerrero, Amy Kim		
		Lupe Guerrero	2 Oct. 1986
89287b	Guzardo, Donna Kaye		
		William A. Guzardo Jr.	31 Oct. 1990

H

Case	Plaintiff	Defendant	Date
8923b	Haas, Tulisha Kay		
		Richard Lee Haas	6 Sept. 1989
89130a	Hagon, Laura Elizabeth		
		Philip Hagon	10 Oct. 1989
CV86104	Hall, Bette		
		J. C. Hall	25 July 1986
CV8750	Hanks, Kelley Ray		
		Catherine Diane Hanks	5 May 1987

Case	Plaintiff	Defendant	Date
89201b	Hanson, Karen L.		
		William B. J. Hanson	22 Nov. 1989
89143c	Hare, Rebecca Ann		
		Danny Dwayne Hare	3 Aug. 1989
CV86301	Harmon, Linda A.		
		Robert D. Harmon	16 Jan. 1987
CV8754	Harris, Toni Lynn		
		William James Harris	8 May 1987
90322a	Harrison, Mary Stella Martinez		
		Hershel Ray Harrison	10 Oct. 1990
8925a	Heidiman, Roy E.		
		Chris Heidiman	21 Apr. 1989
90288a	Helm, Timothy Neal		
		Dinah Lee Lackey	19 Oct. 1990
CV85109	Henley, Arlma Audrey		
		Williby A. Henley	11 Nov. 1985
8951c	Henley, Janice Diane		
		William Karl Henley	24 May 1989
89168a	Henley, Herman Ray		
		Kathy E. Henley	25 Oct. 1989
CV86259	Hernandez, Debra		
		Raymond Hernandez	21 June 1989
CV87294	Hernandez, Diane M.		
		Alex M. Kernandez	20 Sept. 1988
90422c	Hickey, Doris E.		
		C. K. Hickey Jr.	7 Sept. 1990
CV86152	Hill, Gary Randall		
		Peggy Sue Hill	9 Dec. 1986
CV86237	Hill, Rodney W.		
		Elena K. Hill	10 Oct. 1986
9068b	Holison, Audrey Marie		
		Jasper Dwight Holison	30 July 1990
89153c	Hoop, Carl J.		
		Darla Jean Hoop	18 Dec. 1989
CV8848	Hooten, Franklin David		
		Jana Marie Hooten	16 Nov. 1988
CV8665	Horne, Earnest H.		
		Betty L. Horne	29 Apr. 1986
8950c	Hostetter, Kathryn Ann		
		John James Barlow	24 Apr. 1989
CV86281	Howard, Rita Carol		
		David Lee Howard	26 Nov. 1986
89107c	Howell, Marla Daion		
		John Ross Howell	27 July 1989

Case	Plaintiff	Defendant	Date
89119c	Huchton, Laura Marie		
		Timothy Edward Huchton	16 Oct. 1989
89131b	Hufstedler, Paulette Jo		
		Drew Mack Hufstedler	22 Aug. 1989
89165c	Hull, John C.		
		Frances B. Hull	27 Oct. 1989
89205c	Hunsucker, Charles		
		Virginia Hunsucker	14 May 1990
89176c	Hurr, Jacqueline T.		
		Leo Dale Hurr	2 Jan. 1990
9071b	Hutson, Linda		
		Michael Hutson	20 June 1990

I

Case	Plaintiff	Defendant	Date
CV85245	Inks, Roy Banford		
		Eddie Jean Inks	14 May 1986
CV89201	Itz, Betty Jean Bailey		
		Dayton Emil Itz	18 Feb. 1988

J

Case	Plaintiff	Defendant	Date
90472a	Jacks, Robert Earl III		
		Carla Lynn Sharp Jacks	10 Oct. 1990
89276c	Jackson, Constance		
		Stephen Jackson	17 May 1990
CV86246	Jackson, Horace Randall		
		Octavia May Graham Jackson	
			9 June 1987
90295b	Jeffers, Cynthia Sue		
		Donnie Martin Jeffers	11 July 1990
89178a	Jeffers, James William		
		Brenda Moore Yockey Jeffers	
			6 Dec. 1989
9023b	Jobes-Mall, Georgia L.		
		Robert A. Mall	6 June 1990
89158a	Johnson, Brenda Joyce		
		Paul Douglas Johnson	4 Oct. 1989
9089a	Johnson Deborah K.		
		Roger Dean Johnson	24 May 1990
CV87241	Johnson, Opal Maybelle		
		Carl Melvin Johnson	30 Nov. 1987

Case	Plaintiff	Defendant	Date
8974a	Johnson, Susan Joynell		
		Jimmy Dividson Johnson	27 June 1989
CV8773	Johnston, Cathy		
		John Johnston	11 June 1987
89146a	Jones, Anna Jean		
		Virgil Kenneth Jones Jr.	2 Nov. 1989
89123c	Jones, John Robert		
		Jimmy Davidson Jones	27 June 1989
CV87248	Jones, Rickey Eugene		
		Lisa Diane Jones	2 Dec. 1987
8912b	Jordan, Melissa Carns		
		John Edward Jordan	24 May 1989
8960a	Jordan, Raye		
		Bennett Jordan	3 Jan. 1990
90206c	Joseph, Debrah J.		
		Charles E. Joseph	25 June 1990
90122c	Joseph, Leelan Sue		
		John Richard Joseph	12 June 1990
892b	Joyave, Deborah M.		
		Richard Allen Joyave	5 Apr. 1989
CV8731	Juarez, Tammy Jean		
		Reynaldo J. Juarez	8 Apr. 1987

K

Case	Plaintiff	Defendant	Date
90426c	Kardell, Arnold		
		Linda J. Kardell	14 Nov. 1990
CV86205	Kardell, Linda J. Clift		
		Arnold D. Kardell	12 Sept. 1986
CV8687	Kaufhold, Dawn Louise		
		Harold Henry Kaufhold Jr.	
			25 Apr. 1986
90203b	Keeler, Edwin Neil Jr.		
		Jamie Nathoft Keeler	27 Mar. 1990
CV86166	Keffer, Patricia Gayle		
		Jackson Loren Keffer	17 Dec. 1986
8950b	Keith, Kimberly R.		
		Edward L. Keith	24 May 1989
89206c	Keller, Eddie Neil		
		Brenda Lou Keller	4 Dec. 1989
CV88156	Kelly, Denise Cody		
		James Raymond Kelly	25 Aug. 1989

Case	Plaintiff	Defendant	Date
CV8621	Kelly, Sammy David		
		Lucia Elida Kelly	19 Mar. 1986
90319b	Kendricks, William Ernest		
		Sindy Ann Kendricks	11 July 1990
8944c	Kensing, Caron Rene		
		Kenneth Lee Kensing	21 Mar. 1990
CV88192	Kies, W. R. (Buddy)		
		Regina Jo Hill Kies	24 Apr. 1989
CV86206	Kilpatrick, Karen Louise		
		Thomas Loern Kilpatrick Jr.	
			10 Mar. 1987
CV87218	Kirschner, Patricia Ann		
		Robert W. Kirschner	17 Nov. 1987
90386c	Klecha, Katherine Michelle		
		Brian Edward Klecha	13 Aug. 1990
9061c	Klein, Cynthia Elaine		
		Michael Dan Klein	11 July 1990
CV8856	Klein, Daniel A.		
		Jeana A. Klein	5 Oct. 1988
8937c	Klein, Darla Jean		
		Fred Barney Klein	8 May 1989
89174b	Klingeman, Robert Charles		
		Nancy Carol Klingeman	15 Feb. 1990
8949a	Kolacek, Ann Margaret Smith		
		Eddie Dale Kolacek	6 Sept. 1989
CV87324	Kotrea, Ansrea Jeanne		
		Joe Shelldon Kotrea	31 Mar. 1988
CV8870	Kraft, Steven L.		
		Cheri L. Kraft	26 May 1988
89145c	Kruse, Harold John		
		Maxine Maw Hardestry Kruse	
			20 Sept. 1989
CV85173	Krustchinsky, Jo Nell		
		Walter Leon Krustchinsky	9 Apr. 1984

L

Case	Plaintiff	Defendant	Date
CV86139	Lackey, Sherri Lynn		
		Ray Edward Lackey	2 July 1986
CV56212	Lane, Cheryle Lynn		
		Randall Conyers Lane	8 May 1987
CV88143	Langley, Liza Roda Walt		
		Kenneth Dean Langley	2 Sept, 1989

160

Case	Plaintiff	Defendant	Date
8939b	Lanik, Stephen Charles		
		Sabrina Kish Lanik	5 May 1989
90455c	Langston, Elizabeth Ricks		
		Jerry Lee Langston	12 Oct. 1990
89153b	Lara, Alliene Diane		
		Sean Arnold Lara	4 Oct. 1989
90271b	Large, David Wayne		
		Elaine Ann Large	24 Sept. 1990
89181c	Lawriw, Alex		
		Christina Lawriw	5 Feb. 1990
CV86343	Lawrence, Lisa Elaine		
		Timothy Ray Lawrence	26 Mar. 1987
89286a	Leal, Maritere Cavazos		
		Jimmy E. Leal	21 Nov. 1990
CV85105	Lech, Phyllis J.		
		James R. Lech	24 Apr. 1986
CV86203	Ledwig, Wanna V.		
		Joseph Ledwig	12 Sept. 1986
CV87200	Lee, Donald C. T.		
		Denise Nia Lee	1 Nov. 1988
8920a	Leinweber, Robert S.		
		Marie D. Leinweber	3 Oct. 1989
89598c	Leisering, Mark Julius		
		Mary Catherine Leisering	
			20 Dec. 1990
CV87208	Le Meilleur, Marsha Elaine		
		Charles Raymond Le Meilleuer Jr.	
			9 Dec. 1987
CV8877	Le Meilleur, Renda Ann		
		James Donald Lance Le Meilleur	
			24 Aug. 1988
CV8846	Lena, Daniel Burton		
		Gail Elizabeth Lena	30 Jan 1989
8984c	Lerma, Julie		
		Ambrosio Lerma	21 July 1989
CV85251	Lester, William Edward		
		Margaret Virginia Lester	
			30 Dec. 1985
CV87286	Liesmann, Andrea R.		
		Roger M. Liesmann	14 Jan 1988
89178b	Light, Linda Joyce		
		Timy Light	25 Oct. 1989
CV88148	Lopez, Alice Munoz		
		Nicholas Ssanchez	25 Aug. 1988

Case	Plaintiff	Defendant	Date
89199c	Lopez, George R. Jr.		
		Oralia Paloma Lopez	6 Dec. 1989
CV88277	Lopez, Isabel Prueneda		
		Lorenzo Ramos Lopez	27 Mar. 1989
CV85102	Lopez, Manuel		
		Victoria Lopez	15 Nov. 1985
CV86280	Lott, Berthe Mae		
		William Bernard Lott Sr.	4 Dec. 1986
CV86168	Love, Ernest Randall		
		Sheree Lynn Love	1 Aug. 1986
CV87148	Lowrance, Mavis Annette J.		
		Jack Fenton Lowrance	25 Aug, 1987
89263b	Lozano, Maria P.		
		Solomon A. Lozano	4 Apr. 1990
CV87147	Luner, Betty Louise		
		David Eugene Luner	28 Apr. 1987
89217c	Lynch, Jana Dene		
		Harold Ray Lynch	5 Feb. 1990
CV88114	Lyngass, Wanda		
		Bruce Lyngass	30 June 1988

M

Case	Plaintiff	Defendant	Date
89204a	Maguire, Rayne Mc Elhaney		
		John Lester Maguire	20 Dec. 1989
89227b	Mains, Carol Beatrice		
		Charles Lucke II	31 Jan. 1990
CV86223	Makin, Sandra		
		John David Makin	12 Feb. 1987
9023b	Mall, Robert A.		
		Georgia L. Jobes-Mall	6 June 1990
CV8549	Malloy, Beverly Jean		
		Ronald Raymond Malloy	15 May 1986
8942c	Malone, William Carl		
		Alice Margaret Malone	21 Feb. 1990
89117c	Manjarrez, Maria Guadalupe Perez		
		Bernardo Manjarrez	28 Sept. 1989
CV85107	Manning, Robert A.		
		Jo Ann Manning	8 Nov. 1985
CV88225	Maples, Michael David		
		Patsy Dolores Maples	20 Dec. 1988
89230b	Marek, Sandra Leigh		
		Allen Joseph Marek	21 Aug. 1990

Case	Plaintiff	Defendant	Date
CV87162	Martinez, Albert	Adriana Garcia Martinez	18 Sept. 1987
CV8839	Martinez, Frank	Adela Martinez	3 May 1988
9062b	Martinez, Shiela Ann	Joel Lino Martinez	9 May 1990
8965b	Martinez, Walter G. II	Corina Flo Martinez	21 June 1989
89109c	Maser, Shelly Sue	Ronald Dwight Hailey	28 Sept, 1989
89172a	Mason, Barbara K.	Dennis K. Mason	6 Dec. 1989
90462c	Mason, StewardR.	Shirley J. Mason	22 Oct. 1990
90153c	Mason, Terry Lynn	Linda Louise Mason	9 May 1990
CV87105	Massey, Alvin Leroy	Mary Ann Massey	30 July 1987
89254a	Matlage, Joyce Lynn	Edward C. Matlage	6 Feb. 1990
9097b	Matter, April Leigh	Terry Jordon Matter	27 Apr. 1990
CV87153	Maughan, Wanda May	Andrew Jefferson Maughan	16 Sept. 1987
CV8751	Mauney, Patricia	Jimmy Dale Mauney	13 May 1987
CV88174	Mausolf, Gerald Arthur	Sandra Jean Mahula	5 Feb. 1990
8919c	Maya, Alberto Nooueya	Darla Begley Maya	12 Apr. 1989
90594c	Mc Anally, Kennady J.	Donna S. Landritt Mc Anally	12 Dec. 1990
CV8842	Mc Bride, Betty Jim Shelton	Ralph Harry Mc Bride	9 Nov. 1988
89141c	Mc Carthy, Albert William	Cathleen Gail Mc Carthy	20 Sept. 1989
CV87261	Mc Cleary, Wende Lee	John Joseph Mc Cleary	6 July 1988
CV87282	Mc Cracken, Robert Shannon	Elvira Anne Mc Cracken	17 Mar. 1988
90269b	Mc Crory, John	Emma Orman Mc Crory	13 July 1990

163

Case	Plaintiff	Defendant	Date

CV87309 Mc Daniel, Curtis Lee
          Gina Annelle Nebgen Mc Daniel
                                    10 Mar. 1988
89140c Mc Daniel, Kenneth J.
          Nancy A. Mc Daniel   7 Sept, 1989
CV86303 Mc Daniel, Marianne Louise Masters
          Michael Alan Mc Daniel 29 Dec. 1986
CV87239 Mc Donald, Melody Ella
          Zachary Crawford Mc Donald
                                    18 Nov. 1987
90692c Mc Farland, Jo Jean
          Sammy B. Mc Farland   19 Dec. 1990
8959c   Mc Gee, Lisa Fox
          Freddie Carroll Mc Gee 10 Oct. 1989
CV86102 Mc Gehee, Cecil R. Jr.
          Lisa F. Mc Gehee   29 May 1986
90532c Mc Gehee, Christine Marie
          Robert Joe Mc Gehee   19 Nov. 1990
89190c Mc Gehee, Evelyn Kaye
          Lloyd Lee Mc Gehee   16 Nov. 1989
90109A Mc Grath, Mark L.
          Mary B. Mc Grath   1 Sept. 1990
CV86253 Mc Graw, Beverley Jane
          Billy Mc Graw   9 Sept. 1987
CV85252 Mc Kenny, Pat
          Kay Jones Mc Kenny   12 Mar. 1986
90265b Mc Minn, Lisa Ott
          Donald Ray Mc Minn Jr. 1 Oct. 1990
CV865   Mc Naughton, J. B.
          Bobbie Ann Mc Naughton 26 Mar. 1986
89249b Mc Wha, Jamie Jeannine
          William Wayne Mc Wha   21 Mar. 1990
CV87114 Mejia, Alfredo Cordova
          Maria Christina Patrona Mejia
                                    29 July 1987
CV8596 Menchaca, Inez Aguierre
          Robert Menchaca   7 Nov. 1985
CV8761 Mendez, Ceasar Artura
          Cecelia Vargas Mendez   15 July 1987
CV86225 Menn, John Henry
          Johnnie Sue Menn   14 Oct. 1986
90484b Methvin, Parker Burette
          Frances Sweatman Methvin
                                    10 Oct. 1990

Case	Plaintiff Defendant	Date
893a	Mewis, Mary Jeanette Charles William Mewis	15 Mar. 1989
CV876	Michel, Deborah S. Jack D. Michel	24 Aug. 1987
8975b	Miller, Catherine Ann William E. Miller	30 June 1989
90124a	Miller, Dennis Wayne Cynthia Lynn Miller	6 Nov. 1990
CV87274	Miller, Linnette A. Jerry L. Miller	2 Mar. 1988
CV85103	Milton, Linda J. Phillip W. Milton	15 Nov. 1985
89154b	Monroy, Salvador Eva Flores Monroy	27 Oct. 1989
CV88221	Moody, Barbara Gaither Robert David Moody	29 Jan. 1985
CV86354	Moose, John Calvin Reba Jean Moose	24 Mar. 1987
90559a	Moran, Maximo Margerita Rojas Moran	28 Nov. 1990
CV88303	Moreau, Linda Ray Marvin Moreau	15 Feb. 1989
8961b	Moreno, Elias Flores Esther Bill Moreno	9 Aug. 1989
CV8868	Moreno, Lori Ann Raul Bill Moreno	14 July 1988
89191c	Morgan, Pamela Travis Wayne Morgan Jr.	6 June 1990
8928a	Morin, Petra A. Jose F. Morin	24 Oct. 1989
CV85184	Morris, James J. Rosalinda Morris	28 Apr. 1986
CV8579	Mosty, Matthew Arnell B. Mosty	8 Apr. 1986
89161b	Muck, Diane John Kelly Muck	25 Oct. 1989
8991a	Mulliner, Sudie K. Edward Eugene Mulliner	4 Aug. 1989
90186C	Murdock, Willa Reves David Joe Murdock	9 Nov. 1990
89245b	Murell, Margaret Jon Randall Jr.	23 Aug. 1990
89160c	Myers, Dale Tracy Christine Dale Myers	4 Oct. 1989

N

8966c   Nations, Kimberly Worrell
            Wallace Ivey Nations   9 June 1989
CV8783   Neal, Amber
            Alvin Ray Neal   29 July 1987
CV86272 Neid, Becky Diane Belcher
            Donald Steward Neid   22 Sept. 1986
CV86109 Neigut, Wesley O.
            Beverly A. Neigut   5 June 1986
90444b   Nesbitt, David Leon
            Stephanie Denise Nesbitt
                                      6 Nov. 1990
90201c   Nesbitt, Pamela Stone
            Jimmy Wayne Nesbitt   2 Aug. 1990
90118a   Newell, Clifford Sturges
            Jodi Lynn Polidori Newell
                                      8 May 1990
8946B   Niblett, Marion A.
            Rose M. Hernandez Niblett
                                      20 Oct. 1989
CV8792   Nogues, Valerie Mae
            James Carter Nogues   16 July 1987
CV86181 Northern, Karen J.
            Clarence D. Northern   11 Aug. 1986
8968c   Nowlin, Jessie Ercanbrach
            Charles Accy Nowlin Jr.   21 June 1989

O

8965c   O'Brien, Diane Deniese
            Rickey Lee O'Brien   6 Sept. 1989
CV86307 Octon, Sharon Kay
            Gary L. Octon   5 Jan. 1987
CV86159 Oehler, Larry Steven
            Catherine Diane Oehler   14 July 1986
8924c   Orr, William Stephen
            Betty Ellen Orr   13 Aug. 1990
89297b   Osborn, Arthur Levern
            Esmeralda Rodriguez Osborn
                                      3 Aug. 1990
8960A   Osborn, Mary D.
            Jerry B. Osborn   1 June 1989

Case	Plaintiff	Defendant	Date
CV88199	Ottmers, Varnon William		
	Janette H. Ottmers		21 Oct. 1988
8927A	Overton, Terry Wayne		
	Marjorie Ann Overton		24 May 1989
89237a	Ozuna, Horace A.		
	Sylvia G. Ozuna		14 Mar. 1990

P

Case	Plaintiff	Defendant	Date
89123b	Pacheco, Margie		
	Adelaido J. Pacheco		18 Sept, 1989
89211c	Pagel, Ginnetta Louise		
	Thomas Wayne Pagel		20 Dec. 19899
89163c	Pape, Belinda Faye		
	Roger Paul Pape		1 Nov. 1989
90338a	Patton, Susan		
	Thomas Paul Patton		9 Aug. 1990
CV8865	Peck, Dorris Dianne		
	Ronald Wayne Peck		17 Aug. 1988
CV88282	Peek, Jo Ann		
	Amos Earl Peek		15 Feb. 1989
89269c	Pehl, Lynette Kay		
	Wayne John Pehl		11 May 1990
8912a	Peironnet, David H.		
	Lynda M. Peironnet		22 Mar. 1989
CV87210	Pelzel, Vaughn		
	Donnie Lee Pelzel		25 Nov. 1987
89213a	Pennington, Kathleen		
	Carl Pennington		20 Dec 1989
CV88189	Perales, Cheryl Renee		
	Ramon Perales III		13 Oct. 1988
9055a	Perez, Dolores Aguirre		
	Fidercir Perez		12 Apr. 1990
CV8732	Perez, Peggy Susan		
	Perfecto Perez		5 Mat 1987
CV86330	Perkins, Linda Mc Entyre		
	Wiefred Donald Perkins		19 Mar. 1987
CV88238	Perryman, Frances Darlene		
	Stephen Allen		5 July 1989
CV8793	Peser, Jacqueline		
	James Larry Peser		17 Dec. 1987
9035b	Pestana, Jeanette Ann		
	Joseph Pestana		25 Apr. 1990

Case	Plaintiff	Defendant	Date
CV85244	Pfeiffer, Shirley L.		
		Richard R. Pfeiffer	28 May 1986
CV85209	Picard, James Douglas		
		Winona Picard	21 Apr. 1986
899a	Pieper, Linda Farris		
		Benjamin Franklin Pieper Jr.	
			15 Mar. 1989
CV861	Pierce, June Farris		
		Eldon Everette Pierce	20 Mar. 1986
CV86200	Pitts, Bessie C.		
		Kenneth Pitts	12 Sept. 1986
CV86205	Pompa, Fernando Leza		
		Natalie Martinez Pompa	23 Sept. 1986
CV8679	Powell, Carol Louise		
		Brad Powell	14 May 1986
90204c	Preece, Pamela K.		
		Johnny D. Preece	13 June 1990
CV88179	Pressler, Rodney Joe		
		Barbara Elaine Pressler	23 Nov. 1988
CV85143	Prestridge, Douglas		
		Starla Gay Prestridge	15 Jan. 1986
CV88298	Puig, Janice J.		
		Anthony L. Puig	1 Mar. 1989

Q

None

R

Case	Plaintiff	Defendant	Date
90331b	Radtke, Richard Wesley		
		Sharon Lynn Radtke	18 June 1990
CV86105	Ragsdale, Sharon Ann		
		Robert E. Ragsdale	28 Oct. 1986
CV85201	Ramirez, Alma Perez		
		David B. Ramirez	23 May 1989
89180c	Rebakus, Linda Lee		
		Joseph Thomas Rebakus	23 Aug. 1990
89199c	Rekart, Christine L.		
		Ronald G. Rekart	20 Dec. 1989
89155c	Reygadas, Mary Christine Lucille		
		Arturo Reygadas	23 Oct. 1989

Case	Plaintiff	Defendant	Date
90418b	Reynolds, Larry M.		
		Karen Saul Reynolds	12 Sept. 1990
90403a	Rhodes, Phyllis Rachel		
		John Paul Rhodes Jr.	28 Sept, 1990
CV8782	Richardson, Edna Marie		
		Willie J. Richardson II	8 June 1987
9018c	Riggs, Donnie Steve		
		Patricia Ann Mills	11 Apr. 1990
8918a	Ritter, Yvonne Bernice		
		David Robert Ritter	3 May 1989
CV88151	Rivera, Girardo		
		Jesusa Rivera	23 Nov. 1988
89279b	Rivera, James A.		
		Rita May Dominguez	14 Mar. 1990
9017a	Robineon, Deborah Kay		
		Jimmy Earl Robineon	11 Apr. 1990
9042c	Robinette, Larry		
		Debra Joyce Robinette	8 May 1990
CV86312	Robinette, Terrell Wayne		
		Lela Irene Robinette	5 Jan. 1987
CV8781	Rodriguez, Elsa Juanita		
		John Manuel Rodriguez	16 July 1987
8939c	Rodriguez, Patricia Ann		
		Richard Rodriguez	3 July 1989
89232a	Rodriguez, Tomas David		
		Linda C. Rios Rodriguez	17 Jan. 1990
CV85262	Rogers, Darren Pierce		
		Sheila Mae Rogers	4 Mar. 1986
90244c	Rogers, Grant R.		
		Pamela A, Rogers	20 June 1990
CV87328	Rogers, Sheila Mae		
		Darren P. Rogers	24 Feb. 1988
CV86112	Rolig, Shelly L.		
		Bryan Shor Rolig	11 June 1986
CV87247	Roll, Patrick James		
		Tina Barrett Roll	23 Feb. 1988
CV88223	Rosales, Amos Alcorta		
		Yolanda Rivera Rosales	16 Nov. 1989
89292a	Rosales, Melani Lynn		
		Ernest Rosales	22 Aug. 1990
CV86117	Roth, David Emil		
		Sheryl Lynn Roth	5 Nov. 1986
89216b	Rowland, Michael Lee		
		Mary Lucille Rowland	31 Jan. 1990

Case	Plaintiff	Defendant	Date

908b   Russell, Albert J.
        Susan B. Russell   9 Apr. 1990

CV8767 Russell, Joy
        H. Lynn Russell   27 May 1987

S

CV86211 Salter, James Forrest
        Denise Nelson Salter   20 Feb. 1986

8911c   Sanchez, Connie Lorraine
        Jose Luis Sanchez   15 Mar. 1989

9020b   Sanchez, Felecita Sylvia
        Trinidad Martinez Sanchez
                       14 Sept. 1990

89203c Sanchez, Maria De La Luz
        Alefonso Sanchez   6 Sept. 1990

CV87166 Sanders, Mary Elizabeth
        Edward Lee Sanders   17 Nov. 1987

CV85100 Sanders, Mary F.
        Palmer Van Sanders   8 Nov. 1985

CV88260 Sandoval, Rocio Acosta Martinez
        Tony Sandoval   20 Dec. 1988

CV88163 Sapp, Bobbette Lynn
        William Allen Sapp Jr. 2 Sept. 1988

90216b Satterfield, Sandra Suzette
        Charles Samual Satterfield
                       14 June 1990

90427b Scheer, Larell Powell
        Danny Ellis Scheer   12 Sept, 1990

89231b Schmerber, Dilia Reyes
        Steve Guiterrez Schmerber
                       30 Apr. 1990

89144a Schmerber, Scotty
        Chandella Marie Schmerber
                       20 Sept, 1989

8971b   Schulle, Janine
        Robert Schulle   26 July 1989

CV86161 Schwartzenburg, Shirley N.
        James L. Schwartzenburg Jr.
                       1 Aug. 1986

89211b Seely, Wilma Gail
        Richard Lee Seeley   5 Sec. 1989

Case	Plaintiff	Defendant	Date
CV85230	Shackleford, Sally D.		
		Ernest D. Shackleford	19 May 1986
9012c	Shaw, Deborah Jean		
		Mark Allen Shaw	14 Mar. 1990
90362c	Sheffield, Doris Aida		
		Sam Sheffield Jr.	26 Oct. 1990
CV88181	Shelby, Billy		
		Beverly Jean Shelby	4 Oct. 1988
89132b	Sheriff, Linda Mc Graw		
		Dennis Fletcher Sheriff	9 Apr. 1990
89141b	Shields, Mae		
		Frank Benoit Shields	22 Oct. 1990
9041b	Shoemake. Timothy D.		
		Janet R. Shoemake	28 Mar. 1990
90395b	Sholund, Doris Jean		
		Robert Louis Sholund	15 Aug. 1990
90375a	Shomette, Gretchen Marie		
		Timothy Clark	15 Aug. 1990
89272b	Shone, Don Lee		
		Charlene Annette Shone	31 Jan. 1990
9054c	Sieker, Crystal M.		
		Fred Sieker	7 June 1990
90193c	Sill, Laura Kathleen		
		Ronald Eugene Sill	14 Nov. 1990
90339	Silva, Ernestine Trevino		
		Abel M. Silva	15 Aug. 1990
CV85255	Silva, Noe Montelvo		
		Eloise Mendietta Silva	16 Feb. 1986
8940a	Silver, Mary Lou		
		Momar Robert Silver	26 June 1989
90105c	Simmons, Randy		
		Linda Simmons	14 Aug. 1990
CV85131	Simmons, Wanda Ann		
		Robert Louis Simmons	21 Jan. 1985
89114c	Simone, Wyona		
		Paul Dennis Simone	7 Aug. 1989
89214b	Sinclair, L. David		
		Georgia English Sinclair	
			7 May 1990
90352a	Sinclair, Ray G.		
		Jan Marie Sinclair	10 Oct. 1990
CV88112	Sitton, Jimmy		
		Carrie Katherine Woerner	
			22 Jan. 1989

Case	Plaintiff	Defendant	Date
8960c	Small, Carolyn		
		Robert C. Small	20 Apr. 1990
CV88312	Smith, Debra A. Wilks		
		Michael Lee Smith	6 June 1989
CV87299	Smith, Dorothea Angela		
		Tommy Layne Smith	5 Feb. 1988
8914a	Smith, Steve Michael		
		Terri Lynn Crum Smith	5 Feb. 1990
90357b	Smith, Susan Joan		
		Richard Allen Smith	14 Nov. 1990
CV88311	Smith, Susie Jan		
		Walter L. Smith Sr.	5 Apr. 1989
CV86244	Smith, Winford G.		
		Julia Ann Smith	14 Oct. 1986

T

Case	Plaintiff	Defendant	Date
90299b	Taccetta, Joseph L.		
		Tosha Renee Taccetta	15 Aug. 1990
89157c	Tackette, Patty Sue Puillan		
		Lawrence Arlen Tackette	4 Oct. 1989
9065b	Taylor, Eddie Ernest Jr.		
		Billie June Taylor	11 Apr. 1990
CV88228	Taylor, Julia Kaye		
		Randy Scott Taylor	23 Nov. 1988
CV86322	Terrell, Deborah Kay Dodd		
		Mark Anthony Terrell	17 May 1987
CV8815	Terrell, Lillian Marie		
		Billy Don Terrell	7 13 1988
8916b	Thomas, James Robert		
		Marjie Fay Thomas	3 May 1989
CV87127	Thomas, Jerald Lewis		
		Janet Elaine Thomas	25 Aug. 1987
90338a	Thomas, Paul		
		Susan Patton Thomas	9 Aug. 1990
89127c	Thomas, Troy Lee		
		Barbara Thomas	31 Jan. 1990
90211c	Thompson, Dianne Lynn		
		Justin Ray Thompson	2 June 1990
CV85158	Thompson, Donna Sue		
		Stanley F. Thompson Jr.	20 June 1986
89121C	Thompson, Thomas Aaron		
		Connie Lyn Thompson	7 Sept. 1989

Case	Plaintiff	Defendant	Date
9069c	Thornhill, Charlotte Ann		
		Bryan Thornhill	14 Nov. 1990
90387a	Threadgill Shawn Wesley		
		Melanie K. Threadgill	15 Aug. 1990
CV8794	Tipton, Martha Jo		
		James William Tipton	15 July 1987
CV88201	Tober, Cynthia Williams		
		Enrique Trevino Tovar	17 Dec. 1990
CV8637	Torres, Jose Ismael Zacarias		
		Rosalinda Garza Torres	27 Mar. 1986
CV86290	Tovar, Carlos Torres		
		Florinda Castro Troy	8 Dec, 1986
CV87175	Tremper, Floyd Monroe		
		Trisha Teague Tremper	26 Oct. 1987
CV88128	Trinastich, O. Jean		
		Paul L. Trinastich	12 July 1988
CV86204	Troy, Marilyn Anne		
		Raymond Owen Troy	3 Oct. 1986
CV85112	Tucker, Craig Howard		
		Lavois Tucker	19 May 1986
CV88218	Turley, Tammy Lynn		
		Steward Dale Turley	16 Dec. 1988
89260b	Tyson, Evelyn		
		Michael Guerra Tyson	31 Jan. 1990

U

Case	Plaintiff	Defendant	Date
90369	Ubbins, James R.		
		Sandra Neal Ubbins	15 Aug. 1990
90231a	Utley, Marie Lynn		
		Joseph Allen Utley	3 July 1990

V

Case	Plaintiff	Defendant	Date
9043a	Valdez, Catherine Yvette		
		Johnny Anderson Valdez	15 June 1990
CV8572	Valentine, Wanitha Hicks		
		Scott Douglas Valentine	6 Feb. 1986
CV8631	Vandeknapp, Teresa Gaye		
		Robert William Vandeknapp	
			22 Sept. 1986

Case	Plaintiff	Defendant	Date
CV8798	Vandiver, Janet Louise		
		Arthur James Vandiver	16 Sept. 1987
CV8790	Vangarder, Kimberly Ann		
		Randell Cleave Vangarder	
			15 July 1987
89139b	Van Hoozer, Carol		
		John A. Van Hoozer	3 Oct. 1989
89240	Van Winkle, Michael R.		
		Jan Newman Van Winkle	6 Apr. 1990
8922c	Vaughn, Austin		
		???? Vaughn	20 Apr. 1989
CV88286	Vega, Debra Jean		
		Robert Arreola Vega	19 Jan. 1989
89248a	Verona, Nora Sanchez		
		Arthur W. Verona Jr.	13 Feb. 1990
CV87198	Villarreal, Lucy		
		Felix Villarreal Jr.	23 Feb. 1988
CV87258	Vining, Carla Sue		
		Jack Charles Vining	21 Dec. 1987
CV8742	Virgen, Dana Lyn		
		Daniel R. Virgen	14 May 1987
CV87128	Vlasek, Anne C.		
		Nicholas Vlasek	16 Sept. 1987
89205a	Vlasek, Frank E.		
		Robin Ann Vlasek	6 Dec. 1989
9057c	Voelkel, Lee Charles		
		Nettie Elizabeth Voelkel	
			11 May 1990
89277c	Voges, Betty Anderson		
		Harry William Vages	30 Apr. 1990
CV86224	Vogues, Frances Marie		
		Harry William Vagues	4 Dec. 1986

W

Case	Plaintiff	Defendant	Date
CV86306	Wachter, James E.		
		Tammy L. Wachter	12 Dec. 1986
90174c	Wahrmund, Erwin Edward		
		Bonnie L. Pelton Wahrmund	
			29 Aug. 190
89159b	Waliky, Debra Petty		
		Bob Allen Waliky	25 Oct. 1989

Case	Plaintiff	Defendant	Date
CV88180	Waliky, Lisa Renae		
		John Waliky Jr.	28 Oct. 1988
CV86236	Walker, Deblynne Kay		
		Richard E. Walker	21 Oct. 1986
90600c	Wallace, Claudie M.		
		Alvin A. Wallace	19 Dec. 1990
CV8728	Wallace, Frank Eugene		
		Catherine S. Wallace	14 May 1987
8927c	Walters, Jimmy Russell		
		Vickie Lee Southern Walters	
			24 Apr. 1989
89128b	Walters, Wesley F.		
		Julie Kouth Walters	6 Nov. 1989
89268c	Wandlesss, John Finlon		
		Elizabeth Aguirre Wandless	
			31 Jan 1990
CV8643	Ward, Brenda Joyce		
		Cary Louis Ward	2 Apr. 1986
89127a	Ward, Juliette Schulze		
		Christopher David Ward	2 Oct. 1989
CV8652	Weaver, Nancy Jane		
		Gerald Thomas Weaver	6 Apr. 1986
905b	Wedin, Sarah D.		
		Morgan F. Wedin	14 Mar. 1990
CV877	Wells, Karen Raye		
		David Gregory Wells	21 July 1989
CV88107	Welsh, Doria Annette		
		Jerry Todd Welsh	15 June 1989
CV88141	Welsh, Patsy Lonnell		
		Tommy Max Welsh	17 Aug. 1988
CV872	Werner, Allison Britt		
		Ottis Dwight Werner	28 May 1987
8975a	Wheat. Cindy Lou		
		Charlie Joe Wheat	8 Aug. 1989
8946b	Wheatcraft, Joan Lynn		
		Gerald Eugene Wheatcraft	
			7 Mar. 1990
9053b	Wheatley, Larry E.		
		Beth Jane Itz Wheatley	25 Apr. 1990
90505a	Whitcotton, Sherry Mae		
		Jackie Gene Whitcotton	9 Nov. 1990
CV86308	White, Dorothy Virginia		
		James Randall White	19 Nov. 1986

Case	Plaintiff	Defendant	Date

90525c White, Lezlee Frances
      Richard Hans White   14 Nov. 1990
CV86256 White, Linda Kay
      James William White   8 May 1987
90184c Whitton, Brain Justin
      Jennifer Louise Whitton 17 May 1990
CV88129 Wicker, Anna Dolezal Douglas
      Lellwyn Dale Wicker   26 July 1988
CV87235 Wicker, Oleta
      L. D. Wicker   17 Dec. 1987
899c Wilkerson, William Leo Jr.
      Wanda Lorene Wilkerson 23 Mar. 1989
CV86194 Willard, Debra Ann
      Michael William Willard 22 Oct. 1986
90341b Williams, David
      Deborah Williams   23 July 1990
89237b Willman, Lisa
      Donald Willman   6 Feb. 1990
CV85248 Wilson, Constance May
      Robert Lee Wilson   12 Feb. 1986
CV87131 Wilson, Donald Glynn
      Debra Lynette Wilson   14 Aug. 1987
89193b Wilson, Janie Belle
      Stanley Allen Wilson   2 Feb. 1990
89228B Wilson, Michael Len
      Stephanie Evelyn Wilson 3 Jan 1990
CV87155 Wood, Charles E. J.
      Laura Wood   2 Dec. 1987
CV87169 Wood, Lanette Faye
      Lonnie Gene Wood Jr. 18 Sept. 1987
8985c Wood, Melinda Gail
      Johnny Travis Wood   10 July 1989
CV8763 Woodard, Kathryn Sue
      Michael Bruce Woodard 1 Mar. 1987
90446b Woodrum, Brigit Hecklau
      Clarence Thomas Woodrum 1 Oct. 1990
8951a Wools, Terry Lee
      Susan Gail Wools   15 June 1989
90460c Wooten, Susanna
      Danny Mark Wooten   9 Oct. 1990
89261a Wooton, Jeana Dee
      Bobby Don Wooton   5 Nov. 1990
8966b Wyatt, Angela Irene
      Walter Wyatt   23 July 1989

Case	Plaintiff	Defendant	Date

X

None

Y

89104c	Ybarra, Jesse S.		
		Norma Ybarra	9 Aug. 1989
8941a	Ybarra, Elizabeth Aguirre		
		Robert Torres Ybarra	3 May 1989
CV88293	York, Albert Byron		
		Marjorie Marie York	3 Feb. 1989
CV8636	Young, Cindy Lynn		
		Robert G. Young	16 Apr. 1986

Z

89184c	Zamora, Renaldo M.		
		Sargelia Sandoval Zamora	
			18 June 1990
8991b	Zavala, Rogeleo Torres		
		Laverta Jane Nelson Zavala	
			9 Aug. 1989
CV87376	Zella, Adolph Albert		
		Sandra Kay Zella	28 Dec. 1987